Improving International Competition Order

Improving International Competition Order

An Institutional Approach

Christian A. Conrad

palgrave
macmillan

First published in 2005 by
PALGRAVE MACMILLAN
Houndmills, Basingstoke, Hampshire RG21 6XS and
175 Fifth Avenue, New York, N.Y. 10010
Companies and representatives throughout the world.

PALGRAVE MACMILLAN is the global academic imprint of the Palgrave Macmillan division of St. Martin's Press, LLC and of Palgrave Macmillan Ltd. Macmillan® is a registered trademark in the United States, United Kingdom and other countries. Palgrave is a registered trademark in the European Union and other countries.

ISBN-13: 978–1–4039–4790–1
ISBN-10: 1–4039–4790–2

This book is printed on paper suitable for recycling and made from fully managed and sustained forest sources.

A catalogue record for this book is available from the British Library.

Library of Congress Cataloging-in-Publication Data
Conrad, Christian, 1966–
Improving international competition order: an institutional approach / by Christian Conrad.
p. cm.
Includes bibliographical references and index.
ISBN 1–4039–4790–2
1. Competition, International. 2. Competition – Government policy. 3. International economic relations. 4. Globalization. I. Title.
HF1414.C6645 2005
338.6′048—dc22 2004051337

10 9 8 7 6 5 4 3 2 1
14 13 12 11 10 09 08 07 06 05

Printed and bound in Great Britain by
Antony Rowe Ltd, Chippenham and Eastbourne

Contents

List of Abbreviations

AIA	Agreement on Implementation of Article VI of the General Agreement on Tariffs and Trade 1994
CABSSS	Coalition of American Businesses for Stable Steel Supplies
CASUM	Coalition of Steel Using Manufacturers
CLP	Committee on Competition Law and Policy
BGH	Bundesgerichtshof (Supreme Court of Germany)
DIAC	Draft International Antitrust Code
DSB	Dispute Settlement Body
DSU	Understanding on Rules and Procedures Governing the Settlement of Disputes
EC	European Community
ECJ	European Court of Justice
EFTA	European Free Trade Association
EISA	European Independent Steelwork Association
EU	European Union
FTC	Federal Trade Commission
GATS	General Agreement on Trade in Services
GATT	General Agreement on Tariffs and Trade
GWB	Gesetz gegen Wettbewerbsbeschränkungen
IAA	International Antitrust Authority
ICPAC	International Competition Policy Advisory Committee
ICPO	International Competition Policy Office
IISI	International Iron and Steel Institute
IMF	International Monetary Fund
ITA	International Trade Administration
ITC	International Trade Commission
ITO	International Trade Organization
JGTC	Joint Group on Trade and Competition
KMU	kleinere und mittlere Unternehmen
OECD	Organisation for Economic Cooperation and Development
OPEC	Organization of Petrol Exporting Countries
SITC	Standard International Trade Classification

UK	United Kingdom
UNCTAD	United Nations Conference on Trade and Development
USA	United States of America
WIPO	World Intellectual Property Organization
WTO	World Trade Organization

Introduction: On the Way to an International Competition Order

After the failure of the Havana Charter in 1947, the WTO took over the role of mediator for questions regarding trade, except for cases involving foreign competition policy. Even in trade policy the influence of the WTO remains limited, however, because it can neither act of its own accord nor apply sanctions in cases of violations against the trade rules of GATT, as a national authority would. There are no competition policy instruments to deal with international violations of competition that negatively effect foreign countries, such as abusing a position of market control, export cartels, vertical or horizontal limitations to competition on export markets and mergers that effect third-party countries.[1]

With trade liberalization as the backdrop for the GATT rounds, any effective competition policy must be international in scope if it is to deal with growing globalization and the ever increasing number of international mergers. The volume of global mergers and takeovers reached a level of 2.5 trillion US dollars in 1998, five times that of the early 1990s.[2] Owing to the globalization of economies, companies want not only to sell and produce internationally but also to merge. The current controls on international merging are inefficient, which leads to overlapping and uncoordinated investigations. This type of multinational merger is laborious and opaque for firms, since they have to apply for permission separately in each country. Applications in multiple countries means having to deal with two different legal systems, and the national competition authorities are unable to provide the necessary information for an evaluation because of a fundamental lack in international cooperation and coordination. These stumbling-blocks explain why the demand for a global legal institution is constantly growing, and the USA and EU find themselves under immense pressure to better coordinate their merger approval processes.[3] Other issues addressed in the various approaches to competition regulation include state aid, dumping rules, cartels and rules of distribution.

It will not be easy to find a solution for every problem area in international competition. For instance, the USA suspects that international competition regulations would deprive it of its heavy influence on international competition policy, or that a third party could gain more influence. The USA fears a threat to its anti-dumping rights above all else. Japan and the EU in turn tend to support the extension of the WTO's competence. The EU hopes for a restriction on the extraterritorial application of US laws on the basis of the effects doctrine by which the USA uses its national competition law against foreign companies if they have an impact on the domestic market. Japan wants to stem anti-dumping measures in order to ease Japanese exports. The developing countries also support the WTO with regard to dumping. The EU, which frequently implements anti-dumping measures, is very opposed to it on this particular point.[4]

Many authors suggest adding an international code of rules for competition to the GATT. The proposed discussion on competition policy reform for the new world trade rounds in Doha also seems to be developing in the same direction. An important item here is the intention to begin negotiations on international rules of competition. The developing countries refused to enter the negotiations immediately, since they claim to have neither the know-how nor the capacity to pass their own competition laws and build competition institutions. The industrial nations have declared their readiness to support the developing countries both administratively and financially.

This book represents an attempt to work out conceptions for a better international competition order on the basis of the scientific approach 'law and economics'. Chapter 1 presents the dominant concepts of competition policy as a basis for an international competition order and tries to formulate a synthesis. The result is a new neo-ordoliberal approach. The ideas offered in this chapter are intended to serve as guidelines for the upcoming discussions on reform, and are based upon the international concepts of competition policy.

After having lowered the general import duties in the various GATT rounds, however, anti-dumping measures became one of the most important import restrictions on global trade. Anti-dumping duties are on average 10 to 20 times higher than the existing import duties and can be 100 times higher. Chapter 2 analyses the reasons for the strong increase in anti-dumping measures. The goal of this chapter is to show that the welfare benefits one might to expect to flow from national anti-dumping procedures, with the ultimate aim being an optimal international resource allocation, are not a reality within the framework of the current GATT rules of competition. The chapter expands the analysis of the effects of dumping and anti-dumping measures on international competition and resource allocation, and questions the appropriateness of the measures as an instrument of international competition politics. Finally, alternatives and improvements are suggested.

The aim of Chapters 3 and 4 is to formulate the guidelines necessary in order to synthesize the suggested alternatives and improvements into an international competition policy. The basis for this analysis is to be derived from national forms of competition policy that are internationally congruent. In Chapter 3, a synthesis is made of international competition policies. The goal of fair international competition must be to provide for an optimal international allocation of resources and wealth, thus creating a maximum level of affluence. Several attempts to create independent regulations for international competition have already been made.

Chapter 4 summarizes the discussion on reform. The pressing urgency for reforms of the current competition system will be shown to result from the lack of authority on the part of the WTO, and the problem areas of international trade. The first part of the chapter explains the criteria by which to evaluate reform suggestions. A selection of the most important suggestions is presented, compared and evaluated in the second part, and in the third part the discussion on reform and the evaluation are brought together to form a conclusion.

Finally, Chapter 5 offers strategies that might serve as second-best solutions. They may not be optimal for competition policy, but they are politically feasible and an improvement on the current competition regulations. They could act as a back-up should the WTO competition regulations prove unrealizable. The analyses are based mostly on the theoretical concepts of public choice and of the new institutional economics.

This book is also based on several articles published in the periodicals *World Competition* and *World Trade Journal*. The author is grateful for their copyright permission. Among other sources, the author refers here to information gathered during interviews with the International Trade Administration and International Trade Commission, conducted during his stay as a visiting researcher at Georgetown University, Washington, DC, and to experiences gained while working as a research trainee at the EU Commission in Brussels. He also worked at the Eberhard-Karls University of Tübingen, Germany, in the Department of Economics.

1
The Theory of Competition Policy: an International Synthesis

The role of competition in national and international economic systems

Because of the many forms competition can take, there is no universally accepted definition of it.[1] The basic character of competition in a market economy can be understood as the contention between at least two participants on the supply side and those on the demand side. Competition forces the companies to adjust their supply to correspond to the wishes and needs of their consumers (the regulatory function). In a national economic system the desire to maximize profit produces the dynamic in which the raw materials with the best value are used in production. The end product that offers the best value is in the highest demand and is the most produced, which in turn allows the firm producing it the most room to reduce its prices (the allocation function).[2]

Companies achieve optimal success when their costs equal the profits from an additional unit of production. With enough influence – in other words, a lack of competition – such as with a monopoly, the firm will be able to set a price far above its costs. Thus, through dispersed market power, competition forces prices down, towards production costs. Lower prices are then charged for a higher-quality product, both for finished products and raw materials. This increases the benefits to consumers in the case of finished products and the international competitiveness of a country in the case of raw materials, thus indirectly also affecting employment. Competition guarantees that over the longer term only a company that uses its resources efficiently (that is, practise productive efficiency) can stay in the market (the sanctioning function). A successful company must also continually try to gain a competitive advantage over its competitors by offering new products and new production techniques (the adaptation function). Trying to keep a step ahead of one's competitors prevents resources from being wasted and favours the correction of the relative prices of the factors of production.

Competition leads to a fair market remuneration and thus provides the motivation for good performance, which is in turn the basic requirement for productivity (the distribution function), although the remuneration results from the market are often felt not to be fair.[3] Competition provides a lot of leeway for those participating in the market to develop their potential. A company can thus take responsibility itself for its reaction to decision-making parameters, a worker can change his employment, and a consumer has the freedom to choose between many different offers (the freedom function).[4] Where there are many suppliers competing for the same consumers, this automatically limits the economic power of each supplier, making a market-controlling position impossible (the control function).

The competition described so far is in reference to a point in time and is thus called static competition. The dynamic character of competition is especially important for the growth process of an economy, however.[5] Friedrich August von Hayek portrayed dynamic competition as a process of search and discovery, through which things are discovered that would otherwise have remained unknown or at least not made use of. Competition is evolutionary for Hayek,[6] and this applies to innovation in both product and process. Innovation can be understood in this context as the economic application of a discovery – in other words, invention. In the expectation of above-average rewards from the market, an entrepreneur is always searching for cost-effective methods of production and new products for which there is a potential market demand. The entrepreneur makes a risk assessment at their own expense or else analyses the results of external research. The market decides the success of an innovation and thus in the end the consumer or producer that further refines a product has the last say (the innovation function). Should an entrepreneur decide not to bother with innovation and invention, they will be pushed off the market by their competitors (see the adaptation and sanction functions). It is clear that the functions of competition and adaptation are closely connected with each other. If a company fails to adapt its products to the demand structures on the market and the international division of labour, it will also be sanctioned by the market.

According to Joseph Schumpeter,[7] competition is a process of innovation and subsequent imitation. The successful innovation on the part of the pioneering company proves a competitive advantage over other companies on the market who have maintained their old production structures. Above-average profits are won from this advantage, which in turn makes other companies want to copy the invention, or even forces them to do so if they do not want to be pushed off the market. This is how the new, resource-saving methods of production come about, and bring about widespread technological progress and production growth.[8] The innovation and sanction functions thus support each other in dynamic competition.

From the perspective of any individual company, it would be positive to restrict competition. For one thing, when a company profits from an increase in its market power, such as from a monopoly, it reaps the benefits without having to work for it. Competition is also a nuisance, in that it forces a company to constantly better its performance. If it does not adapt to the market and innovate, it must face losses or may even have to withdraw from the market altogether.[9] The state must protect competition in order to make sure that companies cannot elude the competition functions. Are these functions applicable at the international level, though?

Let us first consider the allocation function. As we have seen already, striving to maximize profit guarantees that the raw materials that offer the best quality for the lowest price are the ones that get used (the first allocation function). In addition, the most cost-effective company has the highest demand and can attract more production because it has the most room to manoeuvre with its prices (the second allocation function). This principle must be the same internationally,[10] though there are country-specific absolute and comparative cost advantages (Ricardo's theory of comparative cost advantage). According to Ricardo, even a unilateral liberalization of foreign trade would give the importing country an advantage. Scarce production factors in individual countries would balance out internationally, which in turn would lead to a higher total productivity.[11]

The largest part of world trade takes place intrasectorally, which means within a branch and between the western industrial nations that have similar cost and demand structures, such as capital and labour provisions. How does foreign trade come about even when there are identical cost and demand structures? This can be explained by the specialization of the producers in meeting various demands. Foreign trade as cross-border competition forces the suppliers to orient themselves to international demands and/or to qualify themselves for a market niche. The broad palette of products that result from this process is also a gain in welfare. Gains are also possible digressively, in other words with a reduced amount of production within the framework of international specialization. With the increased demand corresponding to the world market, production amounts increase and thus decrease unit costs.[12]

The requirements for an international system of competition rules are different from those for national rules in one main way. Private companies compete with each other at the national level, whereas sovereign states compete for their share of the international value creation. Just as individuals try to maximize their advantage in a national system, so do governments at the international level. As international actors they represent the collective interests of their companies and try to maximize the welfare and growth of their country by way of national economic policies, and to this end they have economic policy instruments at their command; '[t]he central purpose of competition law is to benefit society as a whole by ensuring that markets operate efficiently, as free as possible from conduct that distorts competition.'[13]

In contrast to the instruments of individuals, national economic policies have a greater effect on foreign markets by way of the changes in relative prices that they cause. The goal of an international economic system must therefore be to set the framework in such a way that the pursuit of profits on the part of private companies and government leads to a maximization of welfare. In other words, the 'invisible hand' of international competition must be allowed to develop optimally.

If the goal of an international competition system is the maximization of world welfare, global economic resources must be applied in the most productive way. This enables the combination of markets and competition within a national economy, but they must be adapted to an international system in such a way that the political and theoretical guidelines guarantee functioning competition.

We have shown that the same functional conditions exist for international and national competition. Up to this point, an internationally uniform monetary unit for calculations was assumed to make prices comparable. In reality, prices are expressed in various currencies. Exchange rates between national currencies are determined by aggregated macroeconomic values. The individual international exchange relations of goods are thus distorted by their conversion into exchange rates. Seen from a competition policy perspective and taking price level stability and flexible prices for granted, this is clearly behind demands for a uniform global currency.[14]

Assuming the goal of maximizing international production of goods, an international system of competition would have to prevent all types of distortion to competition.[15] We addressed the advantages and workings of the market and competition in this chapter. The question that begs to be asked, however, is how the framework of a competition policy order that optimizes market and competition should look. Various conceptions of competition try to answer just this question. Competition systems are based on functional goal–means conceptions. Assuming a certain theoretical basis, they advise us which competition policy instruments to use in order to achieve our desired goal. There are also many approaches to the construction of a competition system, which is why the most important[16] will be analysed in the chapters that follow in terms of their applicability.

The WTO lost its role in competition policy when the Havana Charter failed, which is why many authors suggest adding an international code of rules for competition to the GATT.[17] The proposed discussion on competition policy reform for the new world trade rounds in Doha seems to be developing in the same direction. The intention to begin negotiations on international rules for competition is a step of great importance. The ideas offered in this chapter are meant to serve as guidelines for the upcoming discussions on reform, and are based upon the international conceptions of competition policy. Discussions on guidelines for competition policy have taken place at the international level, especially in Germany and the USA. The German concept of ordoliberalism (associated with the Freiburg School) will be presented, compared and evaluated first. Next, I address the American workability concept of industrial organization and the German concept of feasible competition. The German concept of free competition, the Austrian School, the American Chicago School and the theory of contestable markets will all be addressed in the third part of the chapter. After this follows the evaluation of the concepts presented. This is followed by a description of the newer competition concepts: the neo-Austrian School, the post-Chicago School and the European School. Finally, I attempt to create a general, ideal picture of an international competition policy, as a synthesis of the concepts herein examined, which can be used as a basis for an international competition order.

The ordoliberalist concept of Walter Eucken

Ordoliberalism, also known as the doctrine of the Freiburg School, can be considered historically to be the most comprehensive system theory. The system of the social market economy in Germany was a product of this theory, as were the competition laws and policies of the European Union. Up to the present time, there have been many empirical studies that reaffirm ordoliberalism, and none of the theses contained therein has yet been falsified.[18] Walter Eucken was the main founding father of ordoliberalism. He agreed with Adam Smith and other classical theorists that the market form of completely free competition would create the best market results, and that the neoclassical microeconomic models were out of touch with reality. Complete competition[19] exists, according to Eucken, when the market participants accept market prices as facts and (are forced to) compete according to ability. In this case, market strategies and obstructive competition are then neutralized.[20] Those who follow ordoliberalism do not share the optimism that the market will develop perfect competition without state intervention, however, since it may be in the interest of companies to rid themselves of irksome competition, by means such as price agreements, mergers, vertical restraints and so on, and to secure profits through a monopoly.[21] Individual freedom in the market is a competition policy goal for ordoliberalism, on the assumption that a company will try to abuse its freedom at the cost of others within competition processes.[22] Thus, a strong state is necessary to channel the behaviour of market participants through laws, and to prevent or remove restrictions to competition through intervention.

The concept of ordoliberalism was the first to distinguish between the system of competition and competition policy.[23] The system of competition represents the framework that the state provides to economic actors for their activities. It determines the long-term rules of the game, which themselves are generally laid down as laws. This institutional framework is intended to guarantee economic freedom for the individual. Competition policy, in contrast, can be understood as the active engagement of the state, with the goal of preserving or enhancing competition.[24] The state's constant surveillance of the market for possible restrictions on competition, and intervention in the market if competition is threatened, belong to competition policy. The system has to be capable of limiting interventions to exceptional cases. Euken developed two types of principles to address this capability: one a competition system and the other a regulation of the market developments. According to the regulation principles, markets unsuitable for complete competition should be directed, or the damages and imperfections, to be expected even in perfect competition, eliminated.[25] The Freiburg School has been criticized for its lack of analytical basis, and the resulting lack of useful suggestions and test criteria for competition policy. Some authors have also found the efficiency and welfare goals of competition to receive too little attention.[26]

The classical liberalist conception of perfect competition, such as the model of Adam Smith, and the concept of competition set out by Walter Eucken mostly assume a static competition. Static competition is primarily of importance for short-term price setting, however. The decisive long-term competition process as a constant string of advancing and following the moves of a dynamic competition remains mostly ignored within these theories.[27] Other concepts of competition policy provide a valuable complement.

The workability concept of industrial organization and the German conception of functional competition: the pessimists

The workability concept comes from the thinking of Clark.[28] Basing himself on the realization of the industrial organization research founded in 1939 by E. S. Mason,[29] Clark considered the model of perfect competition to be a worthy goal, but not realizable owing to the market imperfections found in reality. He considered the model to be a 'first-best solution'. Clark saw a causal relationship between market structure and market behaviour in the industrial organization, however, and from it drew conclusions on market results. It is assumed that a certain market structure creates a certain competitive behaviour, which in turn leads to a specific market result (structure–conduct–performance theory). This cause-and-effect relationship is why Clark argues that influencing market structures could increase economic welfare, and thus hopes to reach the 'second-best conclusion' of workable competition. Competition is considered to be workable if it leads to the results desired by competition policy. In later works, Clark even goes so far as to suggest making markets more efficient by having the state create new market imperfections, an example being the reduction of market transparency in an oligopoly, which would make cartel agreements and coordinated behaviour more difficult.[30]

Clark's theory has been developed further by several authors into the workability concept, otherwise known as the structuralist school.[31] In the USA, the main proponents are Scherer, Bain, Markham and Philips, and in Germany Kantzenbach (conception of functional competition).[32] To differentiate the workability concept from the later Chicago School, it became known as the Harvard School.[33] The workability concept shaped international competition policy in a lasting way, and currently dominates the policies of most national competition regimes. The dilemma theory from the industrial organization as regards economic efficiency and competitive freedom is a characteristic example. Only large, market-capable companies can make use of the economies of large scale, take on the necessary costs of research and development, and implement innovations in the market. On the other hand, large companies restrict the potential numbers of market participants, which of course provides fertile ground for restrictions on competition. Behaviourist representatives of the workability concept, such as Scherer, have expanded the connection between market structure and market results identified by Clark in an attempt to address more fully the aspect of market behaviour. The original thrust of the pure structuralists, such as Bain, still exists in a parallel strand of thinking. Both strands work out criteria by which to test practical competition policy[34] for workability on the markets to be controlled. In other words, they test whether or not competition is effective. If not, it is the responsibility of competition policy to restore functionality to competition through a change in market structure.[35]

Market structure criteria provide the market form that is worth striving towards as a norm; such as the number of customers and suppliers, and market access barriers. Market behaviour criteria determine the desired competition policy actions and reactions of the market participants. Price-setting behaviour of suppliers, product strategies, and research and innovation activities are all examples. The criteria for market results then determine the desired economic market outcomes, such as the efficiency or productivity and the technological progress according the cause-and-effect change as determined by the workability concept. Not only are norms and criteria isolated, but they are also applied in all imaginable combinations.[36] In American law, for example, a two-tiered market test within the framework of the rule of reason (weighing advantages against disadvantages[37]) is used as a control on mergers. A market situation test is first and foremost a necessary tool to determine whether or not workable competition exists at all. A sufficient requirement for a competition policy intervention is the failure to pass a second criterion, namely the market result test, which would mean that the results were intolerably deviated from the norm. The EU Commission acts similarly within the framework of its extended structure conduct performance concept.[38]

In the last 20 years, the industrial organization has been extended to a sustainable theoretical basis of the workability concept by way of game theory and the further development of empirical tests. The absolute connection between market structure and market result has been rejected. The typical feedback in a dynamic competition process between structural behaviours and result variables has been taken into account. Market behaviour can also lead to changes in the market structure. Contrary to the traditional conception of Bains, excessively high prices are not exclusively the result of the market structure but rather are also owing to exclusionary practices that aim to create market entry barriers. It is still assumed that the market structure can provoke competition-restricting behaviour, but strict structural determinism is no longer accepted. Structure is understood within game theory as the external determining factors that are relevant for businesses in decision-making. Meanwhile, the models have also been given a new dynamism. Despite further academic development, however, there will always be a structural factor that cannot be calculated either because it is not quantifiable (such as the level of market entry barriers) or because it is only partially calculable (such as the limits of fixed and variable costs).[39]

Despite numerous attempts to make the workability concept more precise and easier to implement, there are still many problems of differentiation and clarity in both the norms and the characteristics. Specifying the relevant market is especially problematic. The market results themselves are not of much practical use, since comparable results would be necessary to make an evaluation. Comparative markets have to be used as a measure, since the optimal performance of a market remains an unknown quantity, but no two markets have the same conditions. Because of this, the workability concept is preferable, with its generality that includes subjective value judgements as norms.[40]

The central thesis of the workability concept, namely that there is a fundamental connection between market structure, behaviour and result, is not always true.[41] Market results for example, can also be brought about by faulty management behaviour or by irrational human behaviour in general. In addition, the requirements placed upon competition policy are different in each branch, and can change quickly owing to technological progress, which would limit market tests to a specific point in time were they to have any credibility.

Despite this critique of the workability concept, there can be no question as to its success in developing recommendations for competition policy based on microeconomic price theory, which would allow the policies to increase general welfare.[42] Since the workability concept is criticized mostly for its limited applicability and general credibility, the criticism applies in fact to the subject to be studied, the competition itself. Competition is an open process that cannot be so easily quantified. The Austrian School is the best instance of this concept.

The concept of free competition, the Chicago School, the Austrian School and the theory of contestable markets: the competition optimists

The Austrian School

The Austrian School has its roots in Carl Menger's book *Grundzüge der Volkswirtschaft,* published in 1871. His ideas were taken up and developed further first by Eugen von Böhm-Bawerk and Friedrich von

Wieser and then later by Gottfried Haberler, Oskar Morgernstern, Fritz Machlup and Friedrich August von Hayek.[43] Hayek was the first economist to include the dynamic character of competition in economics, which he did in 1949.[44] He considered competition to be evolutionary, and saw it as a method for the discovery of facts that would never be discovered, or at least would remain unexploited without it. It could also be called a search. No one can predict innovations in products and processes to any exact degree. The Austrian School thus contradicts the neoliberal theory of balance. In a dynamic process a balance can be striven for but never reached. The innovations are constantly changing the market conditions and thus the balance point.[45] The task for enterprises is to seek out and realize innovations, and their incentive to do so is the reward for pioneering companies from the market. This is how technical progress is realized. Enterprises must be free to embark upon their search for innovative ideas. This puts the onus on state competition policy to assure that the discovery process is allowed to take place without hindrance. Its only job is to provide a framework in the form of contract and civil law, and intellectual property rights. Hayek rejects any state intervention that alters or distorts competition processes.[46]

The German concept of free competition

The German concept of free competition takes up the dynamic, open, undeterminable character of competition as purported by the Austrian School, and, along with the Chicago School, considers the dynamic aspects with the most intensity. It has also been called the concept of competition freedom, and goes back to Erich Hoppmann.[47] Since the process of competition is determined by the actions of competitors, especially dynamic companies, concrete results from competition structures or state intervention cannot be predicted. The clear correlation between market structures and results, as assumed by the proponents of the workability concept, is considered unrealistic by supporters of the concept of free competition. This position is supported by the results of empirical research, which has disproved the assumption of a compelling, systematic dependency of market results upon market structures.

Because competition is a process that cannot be determined, there can be no market results for competition policy to aspire to. In the best-case scenario, pattern predictions may be accurate. Hoppmann uses the idea of free competition from the classical theorists, relying a great deal on the fundamental works of J. A. Schumpeter on the dynamic competition of innovation and creative destruction,[48] and on F. A. von Hayek on freedom and competition.[49] Competition is equated with freedom and thus represents an independent goal of competitive freedom. The freedom of decision for market participants is also seen as a fundamental requirement in order for competition to be able to increase welfare. The dilemma theory of the workability concept is therefore not rejected, but reformulated rather in terms of harmony between freedom of competition and increasing economic efficiency (the non-dilemma theory). The concept of competitive freedom rejects all state interventions that aim to achieve a certain competition situation by influencing the market structure. Just like the theories of the Austrian School, it accepts only state interventions in the competition process that are aimed at preserving competition and competitive freedom. According to this concept, competition policy should guarantee open and flexible markets, and prevent agreements and behaviours that limit competition.[50]

Intervention is necessary, however, if artificial restrictions to competition occur as a result of enterprise or state actions. Behaviours that restrict competition are then to be dealt with, when they are based upon an inappropriate use of power in the market. If such behaviours occur within the framework of normal competition processes, however, they are to be considered necessary. Desirable and undesirable limitations must be defined for competition policy in the form of regulations. The concept of competitive freedom uses market tests in order to determine both competitive freedom and market power. Cross price elasticity of the products on offer or the flexibility of production is used for the tests. In the case of natural limitations on competition, which are understood to include market failures and natural monopolies, regulation regarding competition-establishing exceptions such as state price controls is necessary.

The Chicago School of anti-trust analysis

The Chicago School of anti-trust analysis also denies any connection between market structure and competitive behaviour.[51] In the USA, the Chicago School represents the antithesis of the workability concept, or Harvard School. It is characterized by a market and competition optimism, and thus sees no role for an interventionist state in either market structure or competition policy. The ideas of Aron Director form the base of the Chicago School, and the main proponents of the concept are Posner, Bork, Stigler and Demsetz. They have enjoyed a good deal of influence on the American antitrust policies and laws since the early 1980s.

The Chicago School applies Darwin's theory of natural selection to the phenomena of market and competition. Since spontaneous trial-and-error processes create optimal market structures, products and forms of production, an optimal welfare in the form of maximum consumer welfare is automatically created by the survival of the fittest. It considers ruinous competition, such as dumping to achieve a monopoly position, to be unrealistic since the costs of squeezing out a competitor would be too high for such an unreliable result. Competition can be restricted by way of cartels, however (horizontal restrictions), which from this viewpoint should be the focus of competition policy controls. The Chicago School sees vertical restrictions to competition as beneficial to efficiency. The welfare-reducing effects that may result from restrictions on competition are not denied, yet the welfare-increasing benefits based on theoretical analyses of mergers take such a central position that the negative side is neglected. Mergers increase productivity by way of assumed scale effects, transactional and organizational advantages, learning processes and the betterment of management qualities. Possible restrictions on consumer profits from market power derived from the potential competition from new suppliers (allocative efficiency) are neglected, however.[52] This explains the Chicago School's positive take on company mergers. The most efficient and therefore optimal company size is automatically brought about by competition. This line of reasoning explains why the Chicago School views the connection between company concentration and profit discovered by the Harvard School as an expression of a high efficiency level, rather than a restriction on competition that reduces consumer profits.

Williamson offers a competition policy compromise in the idea of weighing estimated profits against welfare losses caused by reduced competition intensity when a merger is examined – a process now standard. He himself admits that not all mergers increase efficiency.[53] The schools seem to have found a common denominator, since representatives of the Harvard School suggest weighing the advantages and disadvantages, and do not condemn all monopolies as welfare-reducing *per se*: 'These costs of monopoly may possibly be offset, in part or whole, by benefits from scale economies or an increase in innovation.'[54]

A fundamental difference between the Harvard School and ordoliberalism (the Freiburg School) on the one hand and the Chicago School on the other rests in the evaluation of vertical price assurances (vertical relationships). According to the competition policy envisioned by ordoliberalism, vertical restrictions are a hindrance to competition. They contradict two of the constituting principles of Eucken, namely a functional system of free prices and perfect competition, and the principle of open markets for new participants. A prohibition *per se* would be the consequence. Should unavoidable vertical restrictions occur, they would be placed under the supervision of a monopoly commission that would set as-if competition prices according to the regulating criteria.[55] Whereas the Harvard School and ordoliberalism see restrictions on competition that reduce welfare in vertical price-setting, the Chicago School perceives a welfare increase. The latter argues that the consideration of efficiency must prevail in suppliers' efforts at vertical concentration, since demand for their own product would be reduced by a price increase for both sales and service.[56] The producers, so the argument goes, use price-setting as a means to prevent traders from free-riding by shirking their share of welfare-increasing costs of advertisement, warehousing, and guarantees on service and all-inclusive pricing. The Chicago School considers advertisements as providing information, and thus in principle beneficial to efficiency.[57]

The theory of contestable markets[58] complements the concept of free competition and the Chicago School. It focuses on the direction of potential competition. The goal the American group based around Baumol was to develop was a theoretically founded application for competition policy based on the reference model of perfect competition.[59] Perfect competition as a market situation is artificially created here with the absence of market entrance and exit barriers. If a monopolist tries to raise their prices clearly above the average costs of production for example, it becomes worthwhile for other suppliers to offer that product. Should the monopolist then reduce their prices because of the new competition, the new suppliers would then be able to leave the market with temporary profits – or so it is said. This market situation of 'as-though competition' can influence market behaviour just as perfect competition can. According to this concept the market entrance barriers must be kept low and vertical or horizontal barriers such as cartels and dominant market positions restricting newcomers must be prevented.[60] The contestable markets theory recommends a state competition policy of reducing market exit barriers, which in turn leads to an extensive deregulation and the removal of exit costs such as social plans.[61]

Although Baumol intended to create a viable approach for competition policy based on price theory, the concept of contestable markets is not much more than an ideal and an intellectual approach. The fact that potential competition and actual competition can influence market behaviour is disputed neither academically nor in practice, and was recognized by national economists in the eighteenth century.[62] The assumption that barriers to market entrance can be neglected is unrealistic, however. Adjusting manufacturing to a new product always entails costs. The concept of contestable markets has weaknesses as an intellectual approach as well, especially in the assumptions about market behaviour. Game theory predicts that potential competitors will anticipate a defensive strategy from the established monopolist or at least an immediate decrease in price, and will thus rethink the venture if they would gain no competitive advantage.

Evaluation

The attempts by the adherents of the free competition concept and the Chicago School to grasp the dynamic and open nature are commendable, as is the classification of 'freedom of competition' as a value in and of itself. There may be an overstatement within these efforts, however, as is also the case with the Austrian School. Not all possible behaviours in competition are socially desirable or beneficial for welfare. For example, a company might finance dumping with cross-subsidies, squeezing more competitive producers from the market, which would reduce welfare. Even freedom can be abused. Hoppmann has seen this possibility and thus insists on rules of play. These rules would have to be controlled and implemented by a market supervisory authority. Problems of putting the rules and establishing criteria for intervention into practice still have to be solved, however. It would be folly to think that all possible restrictions to free competition could be covered. The actions of all market participants evade clear categorization as restrictive or non-restrictive for competition, as is clearly illustrated by the example of publicized price lists. Determining areas of competition policy for exemption is also problematic. For one thing, the areas are not easily determined and isolated, which opens the way for lobbyist influence. Another problem is that the prerequisites for a market failure over time disappear with technical progress (or sometimes new ones are created), yet the exemption rules remain in place.

The general applicability of the assumptions made by the Chicago School is questionable. The assumption of negligible market entrance barriers doesn't hold for most branches;[63] these barriers can be generally defined as the costs or resistance that a new producer has to come up with in order to be able to offer a comparable product. Market exit barriers are the costs or resistance faced by a producer wanting to withdraw their product, in effect leaving the market. Entrance barriers are differentiated into absolute, individual cost advantages for the companies already in production, high fixed costs (especially in economies of large scale) and product differentiation such as the software standard from Microsoft. The indivisibility of production factors and high fixed costs (including high research costs such as are found in the pharmaceutical industry) are the main causes of market entrance barriers. Besides high fixed costs there are also networks and production know-how that play an increasing role as barriers.[64] The entrance barriers can also become exit barriers, such as the expenditure on production facilities that are usually lost upon exit (sunk costs).

The discrepancy between the analytical instrument of the statistical neo-classicists and their dynamic orientation is another point of critique of the Chicago School. The clear orientation towards the model of perfect competition with the monopoly as the extreme opposite creates distortions in the statements from economic policy and makes the theory immune to attempts at falsification.[65] The same is true for Hoppmann's conception of freedom of competition.[66] The one-dimensional theory of contestable markets is explainable by way of its historical background. The main motivations behind the formulation of the theory of contestable markets of Baumol were the many market interventions of the American government, which created artificial market entrance and exit barriers.[67] The Harvard and Chicago Schools were created because of changing economic conditions. The academic origins of these concepts – the calculation of markets using the newly available computer technology by the Harvard School in the 1950s, and the changes in the political environment for the Chicago School – have significantly influenced the respective outcomes.

Both the Harvard and the Chicago School have had a large influence on US competition policy and regulations. The Chicago School was increasingly able to take over the prominent position of the Harvard School in the 1980s under President Ronald Reagan.[68] Neither concept had a particularly strong representation in the regulations at that time; rather, a case-by-case judgement of the economic effects of a restriction on competition was the norm (the rule of reason). Neither concept was able to claim complete authority because of the complexity of competition.[69] The different conclusions on competition policy were owing to differing analytical tools. The Harvard School was based upon competition behaviour and market results within the framework of studies based on individual markets. Competition policy norms were formed from inductive analysis based on the industrial organization theory. The Chicago School, in comparison, reached its conclusions on competitive behaviour and market results through deductive analysis based on price theory.[70] The policy conclusions of the industrial organization theory (Harvard School) have been confirmed by the findings of modern price theory, however. If one leaves the framework of the idealized traditional price theory and includes search, transaction and control costs as well as insecure decision-making circumstances, market entrance and exit barriers, then spatial monopolies and a clear reduction in company efficiency advantages result.[71]

There is a definite correlation between market structure or market power and market behaviours in the goals of an enterprise wanting to optimize its profits. A monopolist must behave differently from a polypolist if they want to maximize their profits, although the two forms represent the two extremes. Seen in this light the structure–conduct–performance theory certainly has its justification, but a monopoly and a polypoly are still extreme cases. Most markets can be classified somewhere between the two.[72] The market constellations are unlimited, which means that the competition policy case must in practice weigh the advantages and disadvantages. Market entrance barriers also cannot be ignored; depending on the branch they can even be several times the yearly production costs. Human relations, and thus competitive behaviour, cannot be predetermined. Companies are led by people who do not always act rationally; in fact, rationality is not even necessarily a natural quality of humans. Our environment rewards us for certain behaviours when we act rationally, or optimally in relation to the given circumstances. In Hayek's words, rational behaviour is the result of competition, or the market process, and not vice versa a result of human behaviour.[73] Because of this, practical competition policy must weigh the advantages and disadvantages according to each case. The existence of market barriers is also indisputable, and can represent many times the annual costs of production, depending on the branch. It is also an indisputable fact that human behaviour, and thus competitive behaviour, cannot be principally determined. Not every company behaves rationally; rationality is not a natural and inevitable phenomenon enjoyed by everyone. As Hayek shows, competition is an open and unspecific process of discovery. Market situations will never be identical because of the large number of influential factors, making prognostications almost impossible. Competition theory will never be able to deliver competition policy-makers exact directives for making a decision in a specific situation. The politics must therefore be limited to guaranteeing the rules of the game, playing the role of referee for competition.[74] This is, in fact, an essential role for a market-based economic system.

The concept of free competition has to be rejected inasmuch as it demands the removal of all restrictions on competition. A patent, for example, gives the pioneering enterprise an advantage from their innovation for a limited time. Patents are necessary in order to make investment in research and development worthwhile. It must also be possible for a pioneering enterprise to break into existing markets with their new product. The openness of national markets is thus a prerequisite for the functionality of dynamic competition and needs to be solidly incorporated into an international system of competition regulations. The openness of markets is also necessary if the imitators of the pioneering enterprise are also to have access to markets, since otherwise the monopoly created by the competitive advantage will not be broken up after an appropriate length of time. An open market supports competition, since the companies represented on the market can count on new competitors if there is a good potential for profit, and remain under constant pressure similar to that of competition. Blocked market entrance gives rise to the danger that competition will decrease, with market participants either exiting or merging. This could lead to the market form of a monopoly or an oligopoly.[75]

Uncontrolled competitive freedom can also lead to a monopoly and thus be self-defeating. It is therefore important on the international level to ensure that subsequent competition is not restricted. As is asserted by the theory of contestable markets, artificial market entrance and exit barriers must be identified and removed. The importance of potential competition needs to be tested for individual cases for the point in time that they occur. General bans on restrictions to competition are alone not enough. Market structures themselves can lead to a failure in competitive behaviour, such as collective action or failing to offer a better price – a common occurrence in tight oligopolies. Controls on competitive behaviour are clearly indispensable. Conceptual development has continued apace, however, bringing ever more ideas into the field.

Newer developments

The neo-Austrian School

The Austrian School has made a comeback since the 1970s in the form of the neo-Austrian School. Representatives of the latter include Murray N. Rothbard, Israel Kirzner, Gerald P. O'Driscoll, Mario J. Rizzo and Roger W. Garrison. Despite its name, the neo-Austrian School is located mostly in the USA and represents an opposition to the dominant mathematical econometric theory of balance. Competition is for them an evolutionary, creative and thus incalculable trial-and-error process of discovery, just as it was for Hayek.[76] Markets never reach a balance according to this school of thought.[77] The market forces strive for an equilibrium, but competition processes are constantly affected by new conditions within the dynamic, evolutionary system. Microeconomic models of balance, such as those used by the Chicago School, are thus rejected by the neo-Austrian School. State intervention in the market process is also rejected, since the market price used as an orientation for the market participants seeking competition gets distorted and the process of discovery is drawn out as the market forces seek a new balance.[78] Just as in the Austrian School, the state should be restricted to establishing a system framework, giving market forces the most freedom possible to develop. The individual freedom of an enterprise is the means and the end of competition policy. Efficiency is an automatic result of the evolutionary, dynamic competition process – in contrast to the Chicago School – and not a criterion one could use to evaluate mergers, for example.[79] The free market should provide for new competitors to guarantee enough competition to force market participants into the desired dynamic, evolutionary process. Competition policy must make sure that markets remain open. Enterprises already established in a market must not be protected from competition through direct or indirect interventions, as this would make market entrance all the more difficult for new competitors. Thus, we see an overlap with the theory of contestable markets.[80]

The boundless optimism of the neo-Austrian School regarding competition can be seen clearly with the example of a monopoly of resources. Any advantage enjoyed from the monopoly will be short-lived once competition is attracted that uses a different production technique.[81] According to the neo-Austrian School, should competition policy redistribute monopoly earnings to consumers by way of a market intervention, the interests of enterprises in creating a monopoly would abate, which could mean an untapped synergistic effect and thus losses in welfare.[82] Even if the market entrance barriers created by the state are ignored, there are still many others, as shown in the critique of the theory of contestable markets and the Chicago School.[83] Every market entrance comes with costs and the risk of a poor investment. There are technological advantages, in that some products simply cannot be duplicated, and some spatial monopolies exist because of prohibitive transportation costs. Neither the Austrian nor the neo-Austrian School offers solutions to the issue of market power.

The European School in EC competition law

The German ordoliberal ideas have influenced the EC competition rules from the beginning. The problem has been that the ordoliberal School is not an empirically oriented model with analytic tools for competition policy. The EC Commission has just started to develop a new approach to competition based on ordoliberal ideas, themselves based on dynamic industrial organization theory and new industrial economics. The Commission has adopted several guidelines from the EC Court's case-law over the past few the years, and has written several of its own guidelines for competition policy.[84] Nearly all competition theories were thus drawn upon, as well as the latest economic insights. While the Chicago School remained too general in outlook with its deductive approach using microeconomic models, and the Harvard School (the Workability School) was inappropriate because of considerable theoretical weaknesses, the new industrial economics enabled a more realistic, case-orientated approach. With the help of game theory and more sophisticated microeconomic models, new industrial economics tries to deduce the most likely strategic behaviour from companies in oligopolistic situations. The result has been the revival of the structure–conduct–performance approach and the creation of an empirical, case-orientated analysis. A new European School of competition has since become a name.[85] In contrast to the originally stark rejection of vertical agreements from ordoliberalism and the Harvard School, the European School prefers to weigh the advantages and disadvantages on a case-by-case basis (rule of reason).[86] It can generally be assumed that a restriction on competition by way of vertical restraints is acceptable only if sufficient intra-brand competition does not exist.[87]

The post-Chicago School

A synthesis of different competition theories also took place in the USA in the form of the post-Chicago School. As with the European School, it grew out of the demands from administrative justice and recommended action for competition policy. The findings of the new industrial economics, new and modern industrial organization theory, and game theory all influenced this school. The result was in an international adaptation of competition concepts and thus the European and American competition policies. The term post-Chicago School must be understood historically, not theoretically or methodologically. This school developed out of the critique in the 1980s of the Chicago School dominant in the USA at that time.[88] It was expressed in 1992 for the first time in the judgement of the US

Supreme Court on the case *Eastman Kodak Company* v. *Image Technical Service, Inc.* No. 96–16014, D. C. No. CV–87–01686–AWT.[89] From a theoretical perspective it could be called the contra-Chicago School.

The methodological critique of the Chicago School by the post-Chicago School is that the constantly efficient microeconomic market model is too abstract and theoretical to be used for the complex market conditions that exist in reality. An additional critique is the short-term perspective taken by the models of the Chicago School. Those who follow the post-Chicago School prefer models that are dynamic and tailored to specific individual markets, with the capability of taking market imperfections, external factors of influence, and strategic behaviour into account. Empirical evidence and analysis are added as well.[90] Unlike the Chicagoans, the post-Chicagoans can also be considered competition optimists. They believe neither that markets are efficient *per se* (owing to incomplete information and market entrance barriers, for example), nor that dominant market positions are automatically dismantled over time, nor that the market itself will always sanction inefficient economic behaviour. According to the post-Chicago School, market participants that are not dominant are also capable of distorting competition to their advantage over the long term, by unfair competitive behaviour such as dumping. If the market is made up of a few large companies, they do not necessarily act as competitors, and technological cooperation can meld into competition hindrances.[91] Differences between the two schools are also evident in the judgement of mergers. The post-Chicago School criticizes its predecessor for almost exclusively including static allocated effects and increased production efficiency, while failing to address dynamic losses in efficiency that can come about over time with a restriction on competition – such as lost innovation. It also sees that vertical mergers can be a danger in that competitors are denied access to primary products, and emphasizes the danger of producers taking advantage of consumer dependence.[92] According to Lande, a representative of the post-Chicago School, competition law – thus competition policy – must provide the lowest price for consumers, a price close to production costs.[93] Market interventions will then be unavoidable.

In summary, it is important to keep in mind that none of the competition concepts discussed here can alone provide an optimally functioning competition. The critiques offered here are also reasons why competition policy has moved towards a comprehensive concept for competition, coming away from the individual restrictions on competition.[94] Thus, a general ideal for an international system of regulation for competition is proposed in the following section. It brings the findings of all of the concepts previously addressed together and can be used as a model for Doha, even though political acceptance of ideals is often quite low.

A concept of a new neo-ordoliberalism as an economic ideal for an international system of competition regulations

What should the goal of an international system for the regulation of competition be? The options presented by the competition concepts introduced here are freedom, protection of enterprises from restrictions on competition, efficient allocation, innovative progress and the welfare of consumers.

In this context, the broadly accepted view that American and European competition policies have different goals is important. It is said that the USA concentrates more on the goal of allocation efficiency and consumer welfare, while Europe is focused more on protecting competition as a goal in and of itself.[95] We will therefore look into whether or not a conceptual opposition is possible. It became clear in our explanation of the functions and concepts behind competition that it has an intrinsic value by providing the individual with options in how they want to act. Individual freedom is not an appropriate goal given the current differences in political and cultural opinion at the international level. It is quite another matter, however, if freedom is seen as a medium with which to increase national welfare. This concept of freedom as a goal belongs to every market-economy-oriented state already.[96] The means of reaching this end would be the further efficient allocation, protection of companies from restrictions and a dynamic innovative competition as the prerequisite for innovative progress. Consumer welfare is also a means by which to increase national welfare, since a demand that can choose from several offers compels an efficient selection from which to choose as well as an efficient production. The consumer profits thus remain for the consumers and a monopoly profit is rendered impossible. Competition between suppliers for demand falls under 'protection from restrictions to competition', which guarantees individual freedom and not allocation efficiency and consumer welfare. Individual freedom makes the creative process of discovery possible, which then brings innovative progress with it.

It is the goal, then, to frame a system of competition that guarantees protection against restrictions to competition, in other words the rules of the game that will allow competition to develop fully. The protection of competition as an end in itself, as the Europeans see it, is the prerequisite for consumer welfare and allocation efficiency, and is thus the wider base from which to reach those common goals.

Consequently, we have to conceive regulations for competition that guarantee competitive freedom so as to protect enterprises from restrictions on competition. This will secure an efficient allocation of resources and a dynamic competition process, and hence promote innovative progress in order to maximize consumer and national welfare. The conditions required can be found for the most part in Eucken's constituting principles: private property and contractual freedom, market openness, and full enterprise liability. A legal system that makes it possible to do business is the basic condition for competition. Private property guarantees an entrepreneur that they will profit from any success their efforts have, whereas contractual freedom makes it possible to start an enterprise. Liability is a logical extension of the competitive system of incentives. If an entrepreneur is to use their resources efficiently, they have to calculate risk when making their plans. They will do so only if they can count on success with profits as well as failure with profits.[97] All concepts of competition agree on these constituting principles for a system.

Competition is interdependent and dynamic, as is stressed by the Austrian and Chicago Schools and the concept of competitive freedom (see Figure 1.1). It must be assured at the international level that subsequent competition is not hindered. Artificial market entrance and exit barriers must be identified and dismantled, according to the theory of contestable markets and the Austrian and neo-Austrian Schools. The function of competition to sanction assumes that non-efficient marginal suppliers fall out of the market. Direct subsidies of any kind would work contrary to this goal and protect companies from new competition, thus sealing off the markets. Liability for decisions and entrepreneurial risk must lie exclusively with the enterprises themselves; a system that risks and opportunities must also

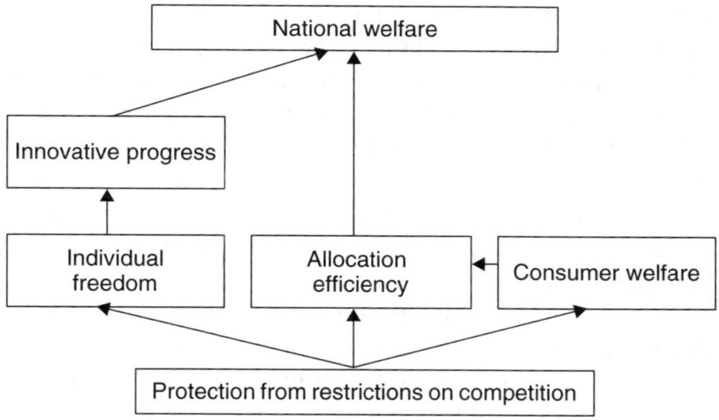

Figure 1.1 Interdependence of competition policy goals

confront. Interpreted narrowly, all majority participation from states in companies must cease, which also applies to the innovation function. Innovations are encouraged when the profits from them are high and calculable for companies. The interests of international consumers, in contrast, are to eradicate monopoly profits that result from innovation. Each goal must be weighed against the other.

That competition regulations provide an opportunity for competition between national markets is a further condition for maximizing wealth through optimal international resource allocation. The demand of ordoliberalism for openness in national markets is an important condition in this sense for the functionality of a dynamic, evolutionary competition based on innovation as stressed by the Austrian School, and must therefore be well established in an international system of competition. It must be possible for a pioneering business to bring new products or production experience into markets that already exist. Open markets are also necessary to guarantee that the imitations of the pioneering company retain market access; otherwise, the monopoly created by a competitive advantage will not be dismantled within an appropriate time frame.

Open markets are also beneficial to competition from the perspective of the theory of contestable markets, the Austrian and the neo-Austrian Schools. The companies represented in an open market can count on competition if they have a high potential for profits, which places them under a similar competitive pressure. If market access is blocked there is a danger that competition will peter out through companies either leaving the market or merging, which in turn would create the market form of a monopoly or congenial oligopoly.[98] Criteria and a legal platform for interventions to preserve market access must therefore be incorporated into regulations on competition. The principle of keeping markets open is universally applicable, and thus open foreign trade also counts as a principle of any competition system.

As became clear in the evaluation of competition concepts, a control mechanism for competition must include market intervention in certain cases. Control is necessary to counteract or at least restrict the negative impact of cartel agreements, predetermined behaviours, price-setting, exclusionary contracts and any other competition hindering or discriminating behaviour. Despite all the optimism, an incentive to limit competition is inherent in the market system. The findings of the modern industrial organization and new industrial economics make this abundantly clear. As a general statement, all concepts of competition besides the neo-Austrian School would be in agreement. Persistent divergence in opinion is to be found over the controls on mergers and vertical agreements. A competition policy compromise might be to weigh the assumed efficiency gained by a merger with the welfare losses from the reduced intensity of competition – a policy that has become the standard. The same applies to vertical agreements.

The international community should set the framework for entrepreneurial activity. The first priority is the laws that regulate market structures, such as cartel and merger laws, and thus serve as a basis for national policy for the regulation of competition. This point is the most contested between the concepts we have looked at, as well as in theories and national governments. On the other hand, the concepts that currently dominate the discourse, the European and post-Chicago Schools, are generally agreed that enterprises and consumers must be protected from practices that hinder competition. The workability concept (the Harvard School) is especially applicable on this point. There must be laws that protect from deception, fraud and breaches of common decency, so that competitive advantages are not gained that are not based on achievement. In order to solve inter-state conflicts, however, it is sufficient if such laws exist at the national level and the contractual partners have agreed on a place of jurisdiction.

Fundamental, thus a constituting principle according to Eucken, is a feasible price system. Prices must reflect the relative cost structure exactly in order for enterprises to be able to recognize affordable primary products. All conceptions and theories of competition are in agreement on this point. An international economic system that maximizes welfare must ensure that the relative international cost and price structures do not become distorted. Subsidies should be prohibited in principle because of the distorting effect they have on competition. In fact, price rigidities should be dismantled in order to adjust the entrance of primary products as quickly as possible in the case of changes in the relative cost structure, which would allow international division of labour and resource allocation to be optimized and general welfare increased. Discrepancies on a common competition law codex exist even in the case of the USA and Europe, however. This is owing to the different economies but also to the different economic concepts applied (in the USA antitrust policy is a goal of economic law, whereas in the European Community competition law is embedded in other legal objectives such as market integration, social policy, and so on). A worldwide competition law or policy concept is even more difficult to achieve because of the differences between countries. Currently, the common understanding is that what is achievable based on Doha is a minimum consensus of antitrust principles.

Limiting influence to making and enforcing rules for competition is fundamental to the expanded ordoliberal concept. Generally accepted economic policy decisions that are directly applicable to particular cases are impossible to achieve owing to the various market situations and the dynamic, changing character of competition. Economic theory can offer only partial analyses for specific cases based on restrictive assumptions, which means that an economic policy oriented towards specific cases (rule of reason) is adequate. It is the goal of an expanded ordoliberal economic policy to allow for the full development of competition functions. The instruments to guarantee this would be everything from market interventions to the breaking up of monopolies, yet the method used must be appropriate for the restriction on welfare or infringement on competition. The main goal is the engagement of all forces of competition to maximize welfare. According to the Kaldor–Hicks criterion, the benefit of the individual may be compromised for the sake of increased general economic benefit that clearly compensates for the effect on the individual. Compensation is an alternative. Intervention in the chances of an individual to develop themselves fully must generally be weighed against the restrictions to competition and the market economy system, since the freedom of creative economic development is the basis of all welfare.

The goal of an international competition system must therefore be to see that the advantage-seeking of private companies and the government leads to maximum global welfare, in other words that the 'invisible hand' of international competition can fully develop. We may call this concept neo-ordoliberalism.

The aim of this book is to work out conceptions for a better international competition order. After having lowered the general import duties in the various GATT rounds however, anti-dumping measures became one of the most important distortions in Competition and import restrictions in global trade. Anti-dumping duties are on average 10–20 times higher than the existing import duties and can be as high as 100 times the import duties. Anti-dumping measures should create and maintain a state of fair competition, taking on the role of a competition organization, which is still lacking on an international level. The following chapter analyses the reasons for the strong increase of anti-dumping measures, which is described in the first part. The second part analyses anti-dumping measures from a competition and allocation perspective.

2

Distortions in Competition: Dumping and Anti-Dumping Measures

The attractiveness of anti-dumping measures, or why anti-dumping measures are so popular

After having lowered the general import duties in the various GATT rounds, however, anti-dumping measures became one of the most important import restrictions in global trade. Anti-dumping duties are on average 10–20 times higher than the existing import duties and can be as high as 100 times the import duties.[1] Dumping is defined in international economics according to two criteria: the sale of goods on an importing market at a price lower than that charged on the domestic market, or the sale on a foreign market at a price lower than the cost of production. Article VI of the GATT prohibits dumping in the international rules of fair trade if it causes or threatens to cause material injury to an existing industrial branch or greatly hinders the development of a new branch (GATT, art. IV). Anti-dumping measures should create and maintain a state of fair competition, taking on the role of a competition organization, which is still lacking on an international level.

The historical development of anti-dumping measures

Despite the fact that anti-dumping regulations were instituted in most countries prior to the First World War, actual anti-dumping measures were the exception until the 1980s. The GATT signatory states handed in on average only 10 anti-dumping complaints in the 1960s, yet in the 1980s the number had already jumped to more than 1600. More than 1000 anti-dumping proceedings took place in the USA, the EU,

Table 2.1 Anti-dumping regulations on record from the GATT (WTO) member states

	1987	*1988*	*1989*	*1990*	*1991*	*1992*	*1993*	*1994*	*1995*	*1996*	*1997*
New users	24	17	19	20	48	70	162	114	83	148	115
Old users*	96	107	77	145	180	256	137	114	73	73	118

* Australia, Canada, the EU, New Zealand and the USA have traditionally been the initiators of anti-dumping procedures.

Source: World Bank (2000), p. 71.

Canada and Australia alone.[2] In the 1990s the number was nearly 2200.[3] In comparison, the volume of world trade increased by more than 300 per cent between 1970 and 1990.

By mid-1996, 776 anti-dumping duties or price restraints resulting from anti-dumping measures were effective for the WTO member states. Two-thirds of anti-dumping proceedings initiated between July 1994 and June 1996 were directed against imports from developing countries. The developing and least-developed countries have meanwhile recognized the value of using anti-dumping measures as a protectionist instrument, and have instituted their own anti-dumping laws and regulations. A clear classification of the victim and aggressor countries for anti-dumping regulations has thus no longer been possible to establish since the 1990s.[4] In addition to the traditional countries such as the USA, the EU, Australia, New Zealand and Canada, countries such as Argentina, Brazil, India, Korea, Mexico and Turkey have all applied anti-dumping regulations (see Table 2.1).[5] How can this increase be explained?

The constructed normal value

The USA implemented its first anti-dumping regulation in 1916, the purpose of which was to act against the 'predatory pricing' of foreign cartels, as opposed to providing compensation for the damage done to the domestic industry. The reforms of 1974 added damage and cost criteria, and in 1979 the Commerce Department took over the competence of conducting anti-dumping proceedings from the US Treasury Department. The number of anti-dumping proceedings in the 1980s increased tremendously because of these two changes. Half of the proceedings can be traced directly or indirectly to considerations based on the cost criterion.[6] The assumption behind the creation of a set of rules governing competition is that cost would be the most expedient criterion to encourage efficient international production. It is only logical that the international company with the most reasonable costs produces the most efficiently. But the question is how costs can be utilized as a criterion.

Defensive measures against dumped imports that conform to GATT regulations include a preliminary and a final anti-dumping duty. In its dumping analysis, the investigating national authority compares the export price with the modified price in the domestic market of the exporting country. Transport costs and total costs attributed to the export of the product are added to the price of the product in the exporting country. The resulting sum is called the normal value. If a product is insufficiently purchased in the home country, or if a normal market situation is absent from the home country, such as in planned economies, one can fall back on the selling price in a third country. If this strategy doesn't prove effective in establishing a normal value, it can also be calculated, which is usually the case in practice.[7]

The mathematically determined normal value for the cost criterion represents the sum of material and production costs, with proportional overhead costs and a minimum profit margin added on (the constructed normal value). The difference between the normal value and the export price equals the dumping margin. After a dumping analysis has determined whether the foreign exporters are offering their products on the import market at prices lower than those on their home market or under their production costs, the injury analysis should determine whether or not this incorrect competitive behaviour has caused lasting damage to the importing country's industry. If damage is expected in the first phase of the process, a preliminary anti-dumping duty will be collected with a maximal sum of the dumping margin, in order to be able to react quickly to the dumped imports and thus avoid damage. Anti-dumping duties in this context are supposed to compensate for the distortion in the competition caused by the dumping of the foreign exporters, since the costs of the export would be raised by the anti-dumping duty to those of the exporter's domestic prices or the production costs. A second phase in the process looks into the possible effects of a permanent anti-dumping duty.

The national authority has significant latitude in anti-dumping investigations. The calculation of the constructed normal value is probably the biggest discretionary cost-calculation issue. The costs involved in the production of a certain product are very difficult to determine. A case of national competition authorities taking action against domestic dumping is an extreme rarity, but when one does occur the cost variable as the measure of the lowest price level (the Areeda–Turner rule)[8] is applied. The term 'variable costs' is also difficult to define owing to the need for exactness in determining what comprises the general costs. Even something as straightforward as the purchase of a machine evades exact calculation, since the depreciation generally diverges from the time of usage. Despite the most complete and balanced methods of calculations, an objective value simply is not to be found for the determination of a fair comparative price within an anti-dumping proceeding.

One would have to assume that in anti-dumping proceedings the investigating national authorities consider the interests of the foreign industry and the interests of domestic industry to be equally important, an assumption which is not especially plausible. Additionally, owing to the fact that the interpretation guidelines for this regulation in the appendix of the current GATT contain numerous exceptions and ambiguous rules, the investigating authority has significant latitude in its investigations. Here are three examples:

1 How the profit margin should be calculated is not included in the regulations stipulated in the current anti-dumping agreement, which creates an artificial dumping situation. This allows the investigating national authority to consider only above-cost sales, increasing the constructed normal value and thus the dumping margin.[9]
2 Strategically singling out selling prices in the exporting country causes a similar discretionary issue. According to current GATT regulations,[10] if sales below production costs comprise more than 20 per cent of total sales in the exporting country, the investigating authority is not required to take account of all sales prices from the exporting country when determining the normal value. This gives the authority two choices: to use the calculated normal value, comprised of cost estimations, or to use only those prices in the normal value calculation that exceed production costs, a so-called 'twisted price criterion'. The USA is particularly fond of this second option. Applying this method causes a distortion in the dumping investigation, putting the foreign producer at a disadvantage.[11] The need

for the cost calculation regulations to be standardized with clear specifications can be clearly seen, as illustrated by these examples.

3 Article 2.2.1.1 requires that all costs documented in the exporters' accounts be part of the calculations for the normal value. National authorities are not obliged to consider these costs if they are not associated directly with the production and sale of the product, however. General costs not directly related to the production of the product involved are habitually disregarded when calculating the normal value (that is, research and development or depreciation). The normal value resulting from the calculations can thus still be underestimated, resulting in an inflated dumping margin.[12]

Another discretionary cost-calculation issue is the choice of information when the constructed normal value is calculated. US policy requires exporters accused of dumping to turn over any information that the American ITA (International Trade Administration) requests for its calculation of the constructed normal value within a rather short period of time. The amount of information requested and its substance have become ever more extensive – to the extent, in fact, that exporters find themselves overburdened and unable to provide the required information. When this happens, the ITA uses the information available (best information available), which in practice necessarily means the biased view of the domestic complainants.[13] This approach throws the burden of proof onto the foreign exporters – to their disadvantage. A new provision to come out of the Uruguay Round was the obligation on investigating authorities to examine whether the exporter was capable of supplying the information required of them within the anti-dumping process. If the exporter seems to have been cooperative, all available information must be considered in the investigation.[14] If the authority establishes the existence of uncooperativeness, it may reject information provided in the questionnaires and may consider the information from the biased domestic complaint documents – as it has done historically. This gives the investigating authority free rein to decide which information it takes into consideration for an investigation.

The attractiveness of the cost criterion can thus be explained by its tendency to put foreign exporters at a disadvantage when it is employed in national anti-dumping proceedings; in other words, to be protectionist. The cost criterion made it into the GATT anti-dumping codex owing to a gentlemen's agreement between the main instigators of anti-dumping proceedings (USA, EU, Canada, Australia) as part of the Tokyo Round, which is hardly surprising if one considers the described protectionist effects of the cost criterion.[15]

Biases of the injury analysis

The purpose of anti-dumping duties is to rectify the distortion in competition that dumping from foreign exporters causes, this being achieved by raising the costs of the export with an anti-dumping duty to match the costs either on the exporter's domestic market or of production. National authorities' injury analyses are not normally meant to determine whether dumped imports have injured the domestic industry at the time of their import. Moreover, the potential to help the domestic industry by way of an anti-dumping duty is a main consideration of authority investigators.[16] It is clear from this perspective that import competitors are indeed in a position to hurt a poorly competitive domestic industry.

As of the Tokyo Round of the GATT, regulations stipulate that the imports under consideration in the injury analysis do not have to be a notable cause of injury, let alone a major cause.[17] It is sufficient for the imports to be *a* cause of injury to domestic industry – among others – for damage to be ascertained. Domestic competition may be the main contributor to injury, or perhaps structural change, recession or even mismanagement; none of which affects the ascertainment of injury. In fact, the injury to domestic consumers as a byproduct of an anti-dumping duty may be worse than the injury to domestic producers caused by the imports. National authorities do not consider this aspect in injury investigations.[18]

Article 9.1 of the current anti-dumping code prohibits anti-dumping duties from being levied to an extent higher than that necessary to compensate for injury. There is no clear method in the agreement for determining the margin of injury. Maximum protection will still be the rule, however, as duties will be levied to the level of the full dumping margin.[19]

We have shown here that, in spite of several improvements, the current international Anti-dumping Code leaves national authorities more than enough possibilities for discrimination against foreign producers. Both the dumping and the injury analyses go beyond a defensive protection against competition violations from foreign producers.

The protectionist effect of the anti-dumping laws is thus undiminished, even after the Uruguay Round.[20]

Additional advantages of anti-dumping complaints

Prusa has looked into the effects of the anti-dumping duties imposed by the USA between 1980 and 1994. On average, the import volume was reduced by around 50 per cent in the three years after the duties were levied. The duties affected the import amount twice as much as it did the prices. On average, a duty of 10 per cent caused a reduction in the import volumes of 1.9 per cent in the first year. This 10 per cent duty also caused a redirection of trade, so that the import of the same goods, just not those in the anti-dumping complaint, increased by 6 per cent in the first year. Where self-restriction agreements or voluntary price commitments were closed, the import volume sank by 60 per cent.[21] Earlier, Messerlin had calculated an import reduction of 40 per cent for products affected by the EU anti-dumping measures taken from 1980 to 1985.[22]

Domestic industry finds anti-dumping complaints to be quite advantageous. They lay open the competition's production costs, which provides the information necessary to create a supply cartel within the framework of the foreign (exporting country's) self-restraint agreements.[23] The domestic industry will most likely decline the offer of self-restraint if it is not interested in a cartel, or wishes to withhold the advantages of cartel returns from its foreign competitors. The US steel industry acted along this line of reasoning in the mid-1990s.[24] The average legal costs of approximately $400,000 per complaint are much less than the expected returns for the domestic producers even if the complaint is rejected.[25] Domestic producers benefit on two fronts. First, foreign producers are deprived of their competitiveness on the US market by preliminary anti-dumping duties, losing their market position. Second, price levels rise when foreign supply drops off, providing American producers with windfall profits. This explains the finding by Prusa, of an average reduction in imports by 20 per cent between 1980 and 1984 even for the American anti-dumping complaints that were rejected.[26] If we consider the US integrated steel producers' annual output of approximately 40 million tons in 1993, an average price increase of just $1 per ton would mean an increase in profit of $40 million. Experts estimate a price increase of $20 per ton as a result of the US anti-dumping and anti-subsidy actions in 1992 and that the American steel producers' legal costs amounted to $40 million, creating a net increase in profit of $760 million.

The importer is the one responsible for paying the preliminary anti-dumping duty, which works like a security deposit; this up-front money is then lost to the importer if a final duty is in fact levied. Should things go well for the importer, they will only lose the opportunity costs. On the other hand, the preliminary duty becomes a financial risk should the importer not be so confident that the complaint is groundless. A shrewd importer will then decline to pursue the business relationship with that particular exporter. Domestic producers are of course aware of this, and have been known to threaten foreign exporters with anti-dumping complaints as a way of forcing an agreement on unofficial export restrictions.

Anti-dumping measures thus increase the risk associated with export business, and create legal costs by way of anti-dumping complaints, not only for the protection-seeking domestic industry but for the exporter as well. The expenses for the Japanese companies alone for their legal support in the anti-dumping complaints of the USA against Japanese steel importers in the 1990s was around $10 million.[27] With this in mind, it is hardly surprising that foreign exporters agree to voluntary price commitments. The domestic producers can use the anti-dumping complaints to force unofficial price commitments, a phenomenon that seems to hold especially true for the USA. Sometimes the mere threat of an anti-dumping complaint is enough. The protectionist dimension of voluntary price commitments is seen in how widely spread it is practised. In the 1980s, the exporters agreed to such a commitment in almost half of the proceedings in order to avoid an anti-dumping duty. There were also parallel price increases from the domestic and foreign producers. The protective effect therefore begins even before the anti-dumping proceedings are set in motion.[28]

Contrary to common assumption, highly concentrated sectors that are weak competitively profit a great deal from anti-dumping measures. The criteria for determining both dumping and damage are central factors. Sectors with numerous national suppliers tend to have intense competition, causing prices to be generally lower than in highly concentrated sectors. Anti-dumping complaints against foreign competitors are then superfluous. Price underbidding from exporters automatically damages sectors incapable of keeping a competitive edge, however. A case for 'damage to an industry branch' can be made with more ease in concentrated industries, by overlooking any damage from domestic competition.[29]

Anti-dumping complaints are especially promising for company branches with high fixed costs, such as the steel industry. This is due to the fact that the foreign producers' export prices are automatically dumping prices caused by the increased costs of producing under capacity.[30] The production costs for branches with a high level of fixed costs vary with the capacity usage. Dumping can also be a result of a below-average degree of capacity usage, as seen in the steel industry. Capacity employment is contingent upon the business cycle in the steel industry. Many steel products are intermediate products for the investment goods industry, hence this interdependence. Should a recessionary phase cause a decline in capacity usage, the steel industry would be forced to raise sales prices to cover fixed costs. Increasing prices is illusionary if demand is already low. The only option open to companies is to sell below production costs as long as the recession lasts, in other words to 'dump'. In calculating a representative normal value for the industry, and ascertaining the production costs for the dumping analysis, the basis must be an entire business cycle,[31] otherwise an 85 per cent capacity usage would have to be assumed. This explains the fact that between 1979 and 1989, 65 per cent of anti-dumping processes in the USA and 53 per cent in the EU were in the metal branch and chemical industry.[32]

The transaction costs theory of the new institutional economics offers another explanation for the dominance of concentrated sectors as plaintiffs:[33] with fewer producers there are fewer transaction costs involved in the coordination of anti-dumping complaints. The interests of the steel-using manufacturers contradict a protectionist policy, since it would increase their consume-expenditures and restrict their product choice, but the high transaction and organizational costs of the many steel-using manufacturers and product consumers for steel prohibit the creation of a lobby interest group. The organizational costs for the producers are conversely much less. There are few producers and many consumers, which is why the profits of protectionism get distributed between few producers and the costs of protectionism distributed across many consumers.[34] The expenditure side of protectionism is difficult for the individual consumers to determine owing to the number of products that are differently affected.[35] This explains why the integrated steel producers of the USA, being concentrated and competitively weak, turned in a record number of anti-dumping complaints.[36]

Countries seeking to protect their national industries from foreign competition need to be aware that anti-dumping duties are not a particularly effective instrument. The high level of administration required by anti-dumping procedures and the minimal protection gained from the duty are clearly disadvantageous factors. Although anti-dumping duties are ill qualified to isolate an entire market, they can most certainly be used as a weapon to keep foreign producers out of a market or to coerce them into an agreement on price controls or voluntary export restraint treaties. The resulting protection effect of anti-dumping proceedings is often underestimated through overlooking these factors.[37] The fact that they are not openly protectionist – as is the case with self-restraint treaties – works to their advantage; with cards well played it may even seem that domestic industry needs to be protected against the unfair dumping practices of foreign companies.[38] Another factor is that reductions of foreign duties have rendered protection provided by traditional import duties negligible. Product-specific safeguard duties have their own problems, since the exporting country is allowed to retaliate with its own measures should it find the safeguard duty unacceptable. Safeguard duties can lead to demands for compensation from the enacting country.[39] This leaves anti-dumping and anti-subsidy duties as the only really suitable protection instruments.

Anti-dumping and anti-subsidy proceedings would therefore seem to be lucrative, particularly for companies in large markets, because the 'return' increases with the size of the market, whereas legal costs remain roughly constant.[40] The same applies to the expenses necessary to maintain an anti-dumping authority. It therefore seems likely that protection against foreign competition increases with the size of a market. Anti-dumping measures as a protectionist instrument are thus mostly applicable for industries larger than states or free-trade zones.

If one uses the concept of the 'new political economy'[41] to explain the behaviour of politicians, and assumes that any politician wants to maximize their own profit above that of the general good, and that the votes necessary to achieve re-election have top priority, one comes to the conclusion that free trade as a means to an end is clearly inadequate. It can in fact have negative consequences. The national anti-dumping measures used by states with the intention of smoothing out the distortions of competition in international trade can end up having a protectionist effect.[42] Not taking advantage of such a competitive advantage in international trade would probably mean short-term unemployment and thus higher social costs for the state, business closures and perhaps a short-term decrease in the GDP. This would likely lead to a loss of votes and perhaps threaten the re-election chances of any politician, since at the time of the vote only the costs of fair competition would be seen, and not the profits to be reaped only over the long term.[43] According to the new political economy, only directly accreditable and short-term causal relationships are relevant for politicians. Uncertain long-term welfare gains of unknown proportions, as in the case of free trade, have a lower present utility for voters in the current election period.[44] The problem is therefore political: it is politically significant whether the competition that squeezes out jobs is domestic or foreign. Politicians tend to favour domestic considerations over foreign in their own interest, despite knowing better than to reject free trade and free market access as fair and equal competition.[45]

Dumping is generally understood as the sale of goods on a foreign market at a price lower than the domestic price or below production costs.[46] Anti-dumping duties are supposed to compensate for this distortion in the competition, since the per unit costs would be raised to those of the exporter's domestic prices or the production costs. The following section analyses the effects of dumping and anti-dumping measures on international competition and resource allocation, and questions the appropriateness of the measures as an instrument of international competition politics. Finally, alternatives and improvements are suggested.

Dumping and anti-dumping measures from a competition and allocation perspective

The effects of dumping

As dumping means the sale on a foreign market at a price lower than the price on the domestic market, it can take place only if foreign and domestic markets are separated (market segmentation), which prevents arbitrage from eliminating price differentials – so that the competition is imperfect. The reasons for market segmentation are a lack of transparency and transaction costs, which might be caused by transportation costs, different currencies, languages, laws and both tariff and non-tariff trade barriers in general.

The effects of dumping are difficult to determine and thus controversial. Dumping generally has negative effects on international resource allocation and competition if financed through profits from other branches of the company, subsidies, or monopoly rents, because in this case the price under-bidding does not reflect the company's performance on the market. One argument for the necessity of anti-dumping proceedings is the detrimental effect on the domestic industry and jobs caused by short-term dumping, so that the importing country suffers welfare losses greater than the gains from the cheap imports. Long-term dumping on the other hand represents a transfer of resources from the exporting country to the importing, and thus a net welfare benefit. Safeguard measures, such as anti-dumping duties, prevent the exploitation of the welfare gains to be had as a result of the low price and the consequent harm to the importing country. To be able to determine the effects of dumping, we have to know how long the dumping goes on. This question can only be answered if we know the motivations of the companies to offer their goods on a foreign market at a price below that on their own market or even below their production costs. There can be different reasons for exporting companies to decide on dumping as a viable practice, and these are now discussed.

Selling below production costs

1 The company can try to increase its share of the foreign market (aggressive dumping), or see itself forced into sinking its price by a dumping pricing advance from a competitor (defensive dumping)[47]. In both cases, the exporting companies must finance their sales below average prices with profits from other markets or other products and will raise their prices as soon as the motivating competition disappears, which makes the dumping short-term and thus damaging to the importing country. Aggressive dumping is the classic case of Viner's[48] predatory pricing. The first US anti-dumping act of 1916 addressed only this case.[49] The damaging effect comes from the exporter establishing himself as a monopolist by destroying the competition through dumping and

subsequently raising his prices. Aggressive dumping occurs rather seldom.[50] In the second case, the exporting company fights for its market share in the importing country by defensive dumping because it expects that the future earnings will compensate for the losses. Apart from that, a retreat would change the previous foreign investments into sunk costs. In both cases, we have short-term dumping in which the importing country suffers, which justifies anti-dumping measures.

2 As production is planned in advance and either fixed costs are unchangeable or capacities may be too costly to adjust, another motivation for price dumping is to compensate for a temporary reduction of demand on the domestic market by increasing exports (demand compensation dumping). In the presence of fluctuations in demand it would make no sense to adjust the capacities. This is also a short-term dumping in which the importing country suffers, and thus justifies anti-dumping measures.[51]

3 A similar motivation is the compensation of a reduction in sales caused by protectionist trade measures on the part of the importing country detour of trade dumping.[52] The time frame of the dumping plays an important role, since the dumping can be long-term if the restrictive measures are as well, and thus have a positive net effect. The assumption that a profit-seeking company will continue to offer its product below cost is faulty, however.[53] The company will seek other markets where it can ask a higher price or increase production, and thus we again have a damaging short-term dumping for which anti-dumping measures are legitimate.

4 The company can gain additional contribution margins, especially by decreasing unit costs (contribution margin dumping). This can take place over the long or the short term, depending on whether it is a tactical, short-term or strategic long-term decision (strategic dumping).[54] If the company plans to transfer part of its production over the long term, it is beneficial for the importing country and an overall welfare gain, but if it is just to increase capacity, the effects are the same as those of a shift in demand. Since the plans of the exporter cannot be determined from an external observer, preventative anti-dumping measures are justified.

5 In order to avoid a loss in sales on the foreign market an exporter may maintain the sales price in the foreign currency despite a revaluation his own currency (exchange rate compensation dumping).[55]

Such a price policy blocks the function of the exchange rate to equalize trade imbalances and disparate levels of competitiveness. The revaluation then holds, which distorts international real exchange relations of goods as well as international resource allocation. The company has to finance this type of dumping as well, since it makes less profit from the exports in its own currency. If the changes in the exchange rate are caused by a longer-lasting trend, the company will increase its export prices sooner or later. If the changes are short-term, the firm will keep its prices steady in order not to risk its market position – all of which makes this a short-term dumping and anti-dumping measures reasonable.

Selling below the price on the home market

1 If the company has a monopoly on both the domestic and foreign markets, and the price elasticity of demand is greater on the foreign market, it will fix the price on the foreign market below that of the domestic (price differentiation dumping). A monopolist sets the price, p, equal to the marginal costs. The marginal returns, MR, are negatively dependent on the elasticity of the demand, η. The profit maximum is reached if the marginal return equals the marginal costs on all markets. This is expressed in the following equation:

$$MR_1 = MR_2 = \cdots = MR_n = MR$$

With reference to the Amoroso–Robinson relation of price elasticity of demand,

$$p_1 (1 + 1/\eta_1) = p_2 (1 + 1/\eta_2) = \cdots = p_n (1 + 1/\eta_n)$$

For two markets, i and k, the following applies:

$$p_i/p_k = [(1 + 1/\eta_k)/(1 + 1/\eta_i)]$$

Consequently, the monopolist sets equal prices on the different markets given equal price elasticity of demand.[56] If the price elasticity is higher, meaning that the consumers will react more sensitively to increasing prices, the monopolist will set the price lower than it is domestically and thus dump. One can assume that the price elasticity of demand remains relatively stable over the long term, which means that this type of dumping represents welfare benefits for the importing country.[57] In this case anti-dumping measures would be disadvantageous.

2 In general, if demand sinks in a market of perfect competition, a supplier has to lower their price. If the demand in the export market is not stable and experiences a downturn, and the exporter expects a normalization of the demand in the future, they will try to remain in the market and charge a lower price than on their home market (demand fluctuation dumping). This is also true in the case of price differentiation as described above with equal elasticities of demand.[58] This is a short-term dumping in which the importing country suffers, and thus justifies anti-dumping measures.

3 If the supplier has a monopoly in his own country, but not on the foreign market, he must accept the price level and adjust his prices accordingly (trade position dumping). Since trade positions tend to remain in place over the longer term, the dumping does as well. This makes anti-dumping measures disadvantageous for the importing country. This shows that dumping is not *per se* 'unfair competition', and does not necessarily have a detrimental effect on the importing country. However, even if it does have a detrimental effect, the negative effects of the anti-dumping measures on the importing country can be higher than the detrimental effect of the dumping, as will be shown in the following.

Can anti-dumping duties balance out distortions in competition?

Several basic weaknesses can be determined when the WTO anti-dumping code is judged according to its role in creating rules of competition designed to minimize distortions in competition.

The criterion of cost as the measure of judgement for dumping

Assuming that the task of a set of rules for competition is to encourage the most efficient international production, cost would be the best criterion. The international company with the most reasonable costs produces logically and most efficiently. The first anti-dumping act by the USA in 1916 was not meant to compensate for the damage done to the domestic industry, but rather was directed against 'predatory pricing' by foreign cartels. The USA introduced damage and cost criteria in their reforms of 1974, and in 1979 the competence to handle anti-dumping proceedings was transferred from the US Treasury Department to the Commerce Department. Both of these changes caused the huge increase in anti-dumping proceedings in the 1980s, half of which were based directly or indirectly on the cost criterion.[59]

Advantage in competition or cost for foreign producers generally plays a role in anti-dumping laws only when a calculation of the normal value of a product based on the production costs is required. The production costs are not determined objectively, however. The investigating national authorities currently determine the costs, and the defendants have only a restricted possibility of presenting a counter argument.[60] Owing to the fact that the anti-dumping code contains numerous exceptions and ambiguous rules, the investigating authority is more or less free to decide which information it includes in its proceedings. Should it decide that the exporter did not behave cooperatively, it has the option of refusing to use the information provided in the questionnaires, and may restrict itself to the subjective information provided in the complaints of the domestic industry.

Furthermore, it is by no means certain that the interpretation of the information will be applied objectively. One might assume that the investigating national authorities would weigh the interests of the foreign industry and the interests of domestic industry, an assumption that is not especially plausible. The discretionary power of the national authorities is significant, owing to the lack of exactness in the cost criterion. The result is that in many cases the dumping analysis determines dumping offences where no dumping has occurred.[61] In these cases, the effects of anti-dumping duties are similar to those of protectionist duties, which is one reason for the international increase in anti-dumping proceedings. Since both the investigating national authority and the domestic and foreign producers are biased by their interests, the cost inquiry should be conducted – if at all – by an independent international authority.

In addition to other variables, the production costs by product are very difficult to measure. In the exceptional case that national competition authorities take action against domestic dumping, they use the variable of cost as the measure of the lowest price level (Areeda–Turner rule).[62] The term 'variable costs' does not lend itself to an exact definition because of the difficulty in saying what exactly comprises the general costs. Even the purchase of a machine does not lend itself to an exact calculation since the depreciation generally diverges from the time of usage. It is clear that despite the most complete and balanced methods of calculation, there is no way to determine an objective value as a fair comparative price within the anti-dumping proceedings.

Anti-dumping measures are meant to create and maintain a state of fair competition. Surprisingly, though, the national competition regulations do not contain sanction mechanisms against dumping in the case of offences by domestic companies. Price discrimination and price differentiation are interpreted here as being the result of market competition, as long as they are not seen to signal the misuse of a dominant market position. To what extent imports can be classified as positive or negative is in reality a political question: the difference between domestic industries losing jobs and profits owing to competition with one another, and losing them owing to competition with foreign companies, is politically relevant.

Injury analysis

National authorities' injury analyses are not usually interpreted as procedures for determining whether or not dumped imports have caused injury to domestic industry at the time of their importation. Rather, the authority investigates whether or not the critical situation of the domestic industry can be improved by introducing an anti-dumping duty.[63] Using this interpretation, it is not difficult to prove that import competitors represent a source of injury for a domestic industry with a weak competitive position.

As has been mentioned before, according to WTO regulations, and even more so since the Tokyo Round of the GATT, the imports under consideration in the injury analysis do not even have to be a notable cause of injury, let alone a major cause.[64] It is therefore sufficient that the imports are proven to be *one* cause of injury to domestic industry – among other causes – in order for injury to be ascertained. For example, the main cause of the determined injury may be domestic competition, structural change, recession or even mismanagement, but this does not affect the determination of injury. On the contrary, the injury to domestic consumers brought about by the introduction of an anti-dumping duty may turn out to be greater than the injury to domestic producers caused by the imports. This aspect is not taken into consideration in the injury investigation by a national authority.[65]

With all of the inaccuracies and huge expenditures involved, it is not surprising that national authorities hesitate to interfere in domestic dumping cases, and begs the question as to the appropriateness of such proceedings. This problem exists in other forms of abuse control that set a certain market price. Such procedures are quite protracted and laborious, thus the better option for competition policies is the guarantee of market structures that make abuse more difficult owing to more evenly distributed market power. Such a constellation would be the task of an international monopoly authority, which as yet does not exist. In addition, the effect of competition remains neglected within anti-dumping proceedings.

Consideration of the effect of competition within anti-dumping proceedings

We saw above that aggressive dumping should be prevented by anti-dumping duties. The main contention on this point, however, is that the exporter can be sure that he will remain the sole supplier only if either the importing market is protected or there are no other foreign suppliers who could compete with them in the market.[66] Unfortunately, this aspect is not addressed in anti-dumping investigations.

In the case of demand-fluctuations dumping, a situation is possible in which both foreign and domestic producer have the same cost structure. If the price falls in both markets to the same level below the minimum average costs, and both adjust their offers, the exporting firm can be accused of dumping in the importing country even though both companies have the same price, market conditions and cost structure.[67] Both foreign and domestic suppliers will have to sell below their production costs. The injury to the domestic industry would be less without the supply of the foreign producer on the market, but anti-dumping measures would be disadvantageous since they could lead to a domestic monopoly or at least impede competition on the domestic market long-term were the foreign supplier to retreat. This aspect is also neglected in anti-dumping investigations.

The effects of competition can be distinguished, as an example, with regard to whether dumping as a price differentiation is based on a monopoly or an exporting cartel in the exporting country. There are two cases to be distinguished here. If the exporter sells below the price of the importing country, because he is a polypolist in that country, but above cost, the anti-dumping authorities in the importing country will impose an anti-dumping duty. In this case, the duties do not compensate for the distortion in competition, rather they just transfer the distortion from the monopolistic position in the exporting country to the importing one. The effect desired by the authorities, namely to make the exporter no longer competitive, is not a foregone conclusion. It will be successful only when the producers in the importing country can produce at a lower cost than the exporter.

In the second case of price differentiation, the exporter sells below his own costs but above his variable costs.[68] In this case, the exporting monopolist would already have financed his fixed costs through domestic sales – through either sales above cost or his monopoly rent. An anti-dumping duty would take care of this distortion. Long-term dumping cannot be assumed in this case since the price calculation and competitive position could change. Had the dumping created a monopolistic position for the exporter in the importing country, the consequent increase in price as well as the elimination of competing industries would limit the welfare benefits. Anti-dumping duties would be justified here as well.

Another possible situation is that a monopoly or cartel exists in both the exporting and the importing countries, which is not taken into consideration in anti-dumping proceedings. Here, the exporter would be forced to raise his price after duties were imposed, whereas the anti-dumping code would have prevented the competition between the two producers. According to welfare theory, this situation is not desirable either internationally or in the importing country. An international competition authority could consider this aspect, since it could observe the import as well as the export market.

Last but not least, a short-term dumping in the form of sales on a foreign market at under production costs can be necessary in a limited time frame in order to overcome market accessibility barriers and make competition under the same conditions possible. Seen in this light, even short-term dumping with a negative effect on the market can stimulate cost economization and thus increase welfare benefits. As long as dumping is not used to force competitors completely out of the market, or create monopolies or oligopolies, it can support an international resource allocation through a comparative cost advantage, something not taken into consideration in anti-dumping proceedings. In this case as well, an international competition authority would be more qualified than a national anti-dumping authority since it could observe and influence the over-arching market structures and behaviours.

Anti-dumping measures as violations of competition

The international anti-dumping law can in fact increase a distortion in competition if the exporter is forced into committing to a price within the framework of an anti-dumping proceeding. If the exporter is not a monopolist in his own country, he will have to join an export cartel in order to be able to adhere to the price. Once the export cartels exist, the transaction costs for the extension of the price agreements to other markets is minimal. If the dumping is not from sales below cost, but rather a trade position dumping, for example, the commitment to certain prices prevents the international exchange of comparative cost advantage.

The protectionist dimension of voluntary price commitments is seen in how widely these occur. In the 1980s, exporters agreed to such a commitment in almost half of the proceedings in order to avoid an anti-dumping duty.[69] The legal character of the current international regulation on competition is clear. A voluntary commitment to a price corresponds to a settlement out of court in which neither the degree of the distortion to competition nor the cause is determined; only the individual economic damages to the plaintiff in the importing country are dealt with.

As mentioned before, anti-dumping complaints are quite advantageous for the domestic industry. They reveal the competition's production costs and offer a basis for a supply cartel within the framework of the foreign (exporting) country's self-restriction agreements.[70] If the domestic industry is not interested in building a cartel, or wants to prevent its foreign competitors from enjoying cartel returns, it will turn down the offer of self-restriction. Such was the case in the US steel industry in the mid-1990s.[71] Furthermore, even should the complaint be rejected, the expected benefit for the domestic producers will be notably higher than the average legal costs of approximately $400,000 per complaint.[72] The benefit for domestic producers consists of two components: one is that foreign producers on the US market are rendered unable to compete because of the preliminary anti-dumping duties, and the other is the reduction of foreign supply, causing the price level to rise and bringing windfall profits for American producers.

Anti-dumping complaints promise to be especially successful for company branches with a high level of fixed costs; the steel industry, for example, since the foreign producers' export prices immediately become dumping prices as a direct result of the increased costs of producing under capacity.[73] Amazingly enough, highly concentrated sectors weaken competition profit from anti-dumping measures. The criteria for dumping and damage are determining factors in this case. There is intense competition in sectors with many national suppliers, which causes prices to be generally lower than in highly concentrated sectors. This makes anti-dumping complaints against foreign competitors superfluous. Foreign price underbidding leads automatically to damage in sectors that are incapable of competing, however. Proving 'damage to an industry branch' is also easier in concentrated industries, since damage from domestic competition can be overlooked.[74] There are also fewer transaction costs involved in the coordination of anti-dumping complaints with fewer producers. This explains why the integrated steel producers of the USA, being concentrated and competitively weak, turned in a record number of anti-dumping complaints.[75]

The separation of competition from anti-dumping proceedings can lead to negative results. The duopolistically structured[76] European soda ash industry was protected by General Direction I (GDI) of the EU Commission (foreign policy) in the form of anti-dumping duties on the foreign industry. The very same industry was hit with a punishment for taking advantage of a dominant market position and price agreements from General Direction IV (competition), however. The GDI even put an anti-dumping duty on the imports from the US subsidiary of both European companies.[77] In the 1980s, in 62 per cent of the cartel proceedings directed against EU companies and 10 per cent of those to determine whether a market-controlling position were exploited domestically, the EU commission simultaneously carried out anti-dumping proceedings against foreign producers.

To summarize, it is by no means the goal of anti-dumping duties to eliminate the cause of competition distortions in the exporting country, but rather simply to alleviate the symptom in the form of damage to the domestic industry. Dumping can be founded, as in the case of a monopoly, on the export market. The anti-dumping duties are directed against the dumping, but the welfare-reducing effect of the exporter's monopoly remains untouched.

Conclusion

The goal of this chapter has been to show that within the framework of the current GATT rules of competition, the welfare benefits to be expected from national anti-dumping proceedings, with the ultimate aim being an optimal international resource allocation, just are not a reality. The recurrence of protectionist effects is made clear through an analysis of the current anti-dumping code, in particular its execution through national authorities.[78]

The many inaccuracies and huge expenditures involved are a good explanation as to why national authorities are quite slow to interfere in domestic dumping cases, which then leads us to ask whether such proceedings are in fact appropriate. There are no sanction mechanisms for dumping perpetrated by domestic companies within national competition regulations, however. As long as price discrimination and differentiation are not established as a misuse of a dominant market position, they will be interpreted as the result of market competition – a problem that occurs with other abuse controls that set a certain market price as well. The procedures to deal with such abuse are both protracted and taxing, so that the better option for competition policy is a market structure that is inauspicious for abuse, and will thus increase the even distribution of market power. An international monopoly authority, which does not as yet exist, would have the task of creating and maintaining such a situation. The effect of competition also still remains to be dealt with within anti-dumping proceedings.[79]

The proven tendency of states to misuse anti-dumping procedures as protectionist instruments, and the fact that dumping within the WTO states is not explicitly forbidden as long as it does not involve the abuse of a market-dominating position, make a case for an international anti-dumping codex in national competition law under the supervision of national authorities with a competence similar to the national competition authorities. The national anti-dumping measures developed historically out of competition law. The American Wilson Tariff Act extended the controls on predatory price undercutting in the Sherman Antitrust Acts ('predatory pricing') into the first law on international trade from and in the USA.[80]

An international competition authority would take the interests of both the domestic industry and the import competition into account with the goal of an optimal resource allocation. It would have privileged access to company figures from both sides, not least of all because no partiality or indiscretion would be feared, as may be the case with national anti-dumping authorities. It could also take action against destructive effects of international dumping in the country from which the exports originated, by controlling or even breaking up monopolies and cartels, for example. This would begin to cure the cause, and not just the symptoms, as is currently the case.

Should an international competition authority prove politically unfeasible, at the least the anti-dumping proceedings will be limited to the cases in which a market competitor breaks the rules of competition to the point that it reduces international welfare. Short-term dumping, and dumping based on a monopoly in the exporting country, would be exactly such cases. One sees here, again, the pressing need for international controls on competition. Reforming national anti-dumping procedural rules so that the real damage to the importing country could be assessed would be highly desirable; here, a distinction would have to be made between suspected long-term and short-term dumping as well as keeping consumer interests always in view.[81] Anti-dumping duties and the costs of proceedings must, of course, never exceed the actual damages inflicted upon the importing country.

We must keep in mind that the number of countries that have used anti-dumping measures has increased tremendously, and the countries that were once those affected by the measures now actively use them themselves.[82] This will lead to more countries not only using anti-dumping duties and protectionist instruments for their industries, but also finding restrictions on their own exports as well. They will have to defend the interests not only of their domestic producers but also of their exporters within the GATT negotiations, perhaps resulting in a more balanced anti-dumping codex. The increasing articulation of import-demand consumer interests, as seen with steel consumers in the USA, is a positive development in this context.[83] Hope remains that other groups in other countries will follow suit.[84]

This chapter has shown that with the current rules of competition in the GATT, national anti-dumping proceedings do not bring about the welfare benefits that an optimal international resource allocation ought. The analysis of the current anti-dumping code, especially its execution through national authorities, shows how the protectionist effect tends to reoccur.[85] A fair international competition based on performance is not guaranteed. Unwanted welfare-benefit-reducing effects of competition are caused by neglecting to consider the potential of these effects within the anti-dumping proceedings.

Messerlin suggests, for example, connecting anti-dumping procedures with an automatic market control procedure through the domestic competition authorities. He hopes to see a deterrent effect on domestic industries looking to protect themselves from imports.[86] Other authors would like to expand objective competition criteria in the GATT anti-dumping code, which would then have to be incorporated into the national anti-dumping procedure.[87] Yet others call for the abolition of both the GATT anti-dumping code and the procedures, suggesting instead that the dumping of both foreign and domestic producers be investigated by national competition authorities. This would necessarily have to include defining the relevant markets, determining the market share and evaluating the price policy from a competition policy perspective.[88]

Dumping within WTO countries is prohibited only in a case where someone wants to take advantage of a market-dominating position.[89] This fact would support the transfer of the international anti-dumping code to national competition regulations under the supervision of an international competition authority, or at least accessible to control through the WTO arbitration committee. If the damaging effects of international dumping were addressed in the exporter's country of origin, breaking up monopolies and cartels for example, the causes and not just the symptoms would be cured.

This suggestion of transferring the anti-dumping code to the national level is by no means unrealistic, as we will see in the next chapter.[90] There are also many examples of trade agreements in which national anti-dumping laws have been substituted by a common competition policy. The best example is the EU, followed by trade agreements between New Zealand and Australia, and between Chile and Canada.[91] However, the international application would probably be nearly as difficult as creating an international competition authority with sanctions capabilities to be used against individual states.

3
A Possible Way to an International Competition Order

After the failure of the Havana Charter in 1947, the role of mediator for questions regarding trade was passed to the WTO, though not for cases involving foreign competition policy. The influence of the WTO is limited even in trade policy, however, because neither can it decide of its own accord to act, nor does it have the ability to apply sanctions in the case of violations against the trade rules of the GATT, as a national authority would. Competition policy instruments to deal with international violations of competition that effect foreign countries negatively – such as taking advantage of a position of market control or export cartels, or vertical and horizontal limitations on competition on export markets and mergers that effect third-party countries – do not exist.[1]

With the background of the trade liberalization in the framework of the GATT rounds, the increasing globalization and the increase in international mergers, a competition policy must also be international. The volume of transactions of the global mergers and takeovers reached a level in 1998 five times that of the early 1990s, with US$2.5 trillion.[2] Because of the globalization of the economy, companies not only want to sell and produce internationally, they also want to merge. In addition, the current controls on international merging are inefficient, which leads to overlapping investigations not coordinated with each other. Such multinational mergers are laborious and opaque for the firms, since they have to apply for permission separately in each country. By doing so, they are obliged to deal with two different legal systems, and the national competition authorities are unable to provide the necessary information for an evaluation because of a fundamental lack in international cooperation and coordination. All of this makes the demand for a global legal institution ever more persistent, and the USA and the EU are under immense pressure to better coordinate their merger approval processes.[3] Many authors suggest adding to the GATT an international code of rules for competition. The proposed discussion on competition policy reform for the new world trade rounds in Doha also seems to be developing in the same direction. The intention to begin negotiations on international rules of competition is decisive, however.

This chapter uses current national competition policies to formulate the guidelines necessary to synthesize them into an international competition policy. The first part addresses the most important restrictions on competition, points out the international similarities and differences in national competition policies, and combines this information with competition theory as a synthesis to produce a suitable strategy for competition policy on the international level. The second part discusses the advantages and disadvantages of an international institution for competition based on the current academic discussion. In closing, the third part derives the necessary institutions for an international competition order.

Synthesis of international competition policies

Cartels

Agreements between market competitors with the same level of added value that restrict competition, so-called horizontal agreements such as cartels, are addressed by all national competition authorities, but treated differently. The prohibition principle (rule of law) and the abuse principle are possible instruments for competition policy. The advantage of a prohibition on principle is its transparency, or legal security, and the policy-relevant prevention of the welfare-reducing effect from cartels. Cartels are sometimes credited with partially positive market (and thus welfare) effects, however, which is why exceptional cases are a part of many national competition policies. In the EU, for example, stemming from a general prohibition from General Direction III, cartels are approved after ascertaining and weighing the effects of individual and group releases.[4] Exceptions to the general prohibition on cartels cannot be explained with competition theory.

Most states try to prevent monopolies and cartels domestically for reasons of competition policy, but may encourage them if they seem to help to increase export competitiveness.[5] This is also why domestic cartels are prohibited in many national competition regulations but export cartels are allowed.[6] Export cartels aim to create monopoly profits at the expense of the foreign countries, and thus not only represent welfare-reducing restrictions on competition but also bring disadvantages for international distribution and promote free-rider behaviour with respect to the public good of free trade. A reform of the international system of competition regulations must therefore have a prohibition on export cartels *per se*.

International consensus has at least been reached on the prohibition of hard-core cartels.[7] Most of the reform strategies suggested in the current reform debate are based on this assumption.[8] The majority of national competition systems allows certain forms of cartels. An international prohibition on cartels *per se* that did not provide for exceptions would thus be politically very difficult to implement. An exception for specific cases is also economically reasonable if a restriction on competition due to only a little market power on the part of the company involved can be ruled out.[9] The rule of reason – weighing the possible efficiency advantages against the welfare disadvantages in the face of a restriction to competition – is used internationally for all non-cartel forms of horizontal cooperation, such as in research.[10] A strategic solution would be to allow exceptions to a prohibition *per se*, which would be subjected to individual scrutiny from an international competition authority. Such an institution could then weigh the arguments offered by the applicants against the expected effects on competition and welfare according to the rule of reason (weighing the advantages and disadvantages of an amalgamation),[11] which corresponds to the neo-ordoliberal concept that has been developed here. The exception would have a set duration, so that the hurdle of getting approval would have to be repeatedly overcome. The effects of the exception would also be better judged over time. Were the expected efficiency gains not realized, or were the negative effects on competition to increase, leading to complaints from consumers, a renewed exception would be very difficult to achieve.[12]

Abuse supervisory authority

The European Court of Justice (ECJ) defines market dominance based on art. 82 of the EC treaty as follows:

> [A] position of economic strength . . . which enables [a firm] to prevent effective competition being maintained on the relevant market by affording it the power to behave to an appreciable extent independently of its competitors, customers and ultimately of its consumers.[13]

In most national competition systems a dominant market position is defined by 'exploitive behaviour', so that the market position makes possible fixed prices above the market level under normal circumstances.[14] The so-called abuse supervisory authority has the goal of protecting competitors on economic levels both above and below that of the cartel from obstructions unrelated to performance and from exploitation in competition. Abuse controls are a normal part of national competition policy and are widespread. Placing a company under a supervisory authority assumes proof of a market-controlling position on the relevant market in all national competition laws. The requirements for this, besides the demarcation of the relevant market, are determining the market share and investigating the competition situation in that market. Monitoring a market-controlling position requires control over the competitive behaviour of the controlling company.

Possible sanctions for an established abuse in national competition laws are omission decrees, monetary penalties, breakups or even jail sentences. Originally the USA led the breaking up of cartels. However, American competition courts now establish market-dominating positions relatively seldom in comparison with those of the EU. There are also certain differences in international interpretations.[15] The shares that the EU uses as the lowest parameter for a market-dominating position vary, according to the market, between 45 and 70 per cent.[16] Markets in the USA tend to be more widely demarcated and most courts consider a dominant position to begin with a 70 per cent market share, which is why a market-dominating position is more rarely established there. These large variations in the market share considered to be dominant show that generally accepted and clear guidelines are not yet possible. A position halfway between those of the

European and American competition authorities in recent times can be established, however, provided the initial conditions are similar.[17]

The abuse of a dominant market position can be dealt with as a criminal act in the USA,[18] whereas the EU Commission can only impose fines. Bridgeman reads from this that the USA can afford to be more lenient[19] on mergers than the EU[20] because of the tougher US sanctions in the case of an abuse. The USA uses a two-level market test within the framework of the so-called rule of reason for merger controls, for example. A market situation test should as a necessary condition clarify whether or not a functional competition exists. In order for the conditions to call for competition policy intervention, the second test criterion must come out negative. In other words, the market results must not diverge beyond a reasonable distance from the norm. The EU Commission acts similarly within the framework of its 'extended structure–conduct–performance' theory.[21]

The abuse authority can also be used for cartels tolerated by states. In Germany, Canada and the Netherlands, the abuse principle also applies to cartels exempt from the prohibition *per se*. In Great Britain, Denmark, Norway and Switzerland it is even applied to hard-core cartels, such as price, quota, submission and market distribution cartels.[22] The abuse authority is confined to proven abuses of sufficient market power, however.

Criteria for a competitive abuse of power

Market tests, in addition to determining the market share, are conducted in order to determine whether a market-dominating position exists. Different criteria are determined according to the Harvard School: market structure, market behaviour and market performance tests. Criteria for the market structure tests, used in order to estimate whether or not sufficient competition takes place, include the number and size of competitors, the possibility of market entrance from a third party,[23] and the degree of market transparency. These criteria are applied differently internationally, mostly owing to their number and inexactness. The same applies for the market behaviour test, although the criteria could be the same pricing behaviour of market competitors and the absence of price-setting behaviour of the consumers. The goal of market performance tests is to determine whether the quality and amount of goods is in relation to their price, thus whether or not the market situation reflects that of competition and whether the prices develop as they would under the patterns attributed to normal market and competition conditions. Market situation and market behaviour tests build the basis for controls on the abuse of an established market-dominating position. The interpretation and application of these instruments are unfortunately very subjective. This is particularly clear, in relation to the market situation test, from an analysis of the use of national anti-dumping measures.[24] It is virtually impossible to find an objective measure for the costs, and thus the price calculations, of a company. Neither can we establish applicable market situations using the comparative market concept, owing to the differences between markets and companies.[25] There are not even any standardized criteria to determine the market position of companies on the national level, since with the flexibility of interpretation the relevant markets can be narrowly or broadly defined. Up to now there have been no objective standards with which to measure the degree of a market access restriction, for example, or the intensity of involvement between companies.

If a dominant market position can be determined despite the above-mentioned difficulties, the abuse of this position must also be determined. Abuse can take the form of discrimination, obstruction or exploitation. Exploitation in this context is the discrimination against market competition through price-setting, in other words maximizing the monopoly or cartel profits. Exploitation abuse, in contrast to obstruction abuse, is mostly effective against suppliers and buyers.[26] In order to determine exploitation, it is imperative to draw on parameters of action from markets with exploitation-free competition as a measure of comparison. This is problematic, however, since market situations are never identical. The latitude of an administration in measuring is thus increased, and with it arbitrary interventions. It is, on the other hand, just as necessary to ensure that competition laws do not lose their effectiveness because of inactivity on the part of the authorities.

There is an extraterritorial problem at the international level, especially for exploitation abuses, since the country of the monopolist has very little incentive to stop the exploitation of foreign consumers[27] but, rather, is likely to see it as a chance to maximize its own welfare through rent-seeking at the cost of the other country.

The maximization of the market position profits in the case of obstruction abuses occurs only indirectly by way of a reduction in competition; for example, in the restriction of market entrance through exclusion agreements, linking agreements and discount practices. Besides defining the market, the formulation of criteria for intervention poses a problem. The motives of a company cannot be determined from outside, and the criteria for the obstruction of competition are determinable only under consideration of competition behavioural norms in the sense of a law against dishonest competition. Thus Germany, for example, puts a stop to the effects of the abuse in case of a proven restriction to competition. The Act Against Restraints on Competition (ARC) therefore considers it an abuse when 'a market dominating company . . . impedes the competitive potential of other companies as regards their competition on the market without a factually justified reason' (s. 22, para. 4, line 2, no. 1 ARC).

Dumping as an abuse of a market-dominating position

According to the German definition of abuse, dumping – understood to be the assumed sale of goods below cost – represents an obstruction to competition without a factually justified reason. The sale of goods on another (foreign) market at a lower price than on one's own domestic market would be an obstruction abuse as well. In both cases, however, a market-dominating position on the part of the dumping company would have to be proven in order for it to be censured as an abuse. Anti-dumping measures would thus be reduced to curbing the specific hindrance to competition and all dumping cases would fall through the cracks except those of market position dumping, price differentiation and aggressive dumping.[28] Aggressive dumping aims to create a monopolistic position in the foreign country by selling below production costs. An international market-dominating position would necessarily be present in this form of international obstruction abuse through price dumping, since other foreign suppliers would otherwise take the place of the displaced domestic supplier. The American definition of abuse reflects this focus as well, and prohibits behaviours that 'substantially lessen competition, or tend to create a monopoly'.[29]

In order to determine the market position of the exporter in the market of the importing country, competition policy has to cross borders. Not only the domestic suppliers and the exporter must be taken into account, but other actual and potential suppliers as well. To complete the competition analysis, the competition authority in the exporting country has to cooperate with the competition authority of the importing country. The goal of the dumping, namely the crowding out of competitors on the domestic market, could be looked into more effectively with the support of the competition authority in the exporting country and thus better assessed than it would be by the authorities in the importing country, since the relevant internal documents from the company would be accessible. Cross-subsidies, the financing of dumping by way of other company branches or products, would also be able to be detected and assessed.

Market position dumping and price differentiation actually represent an advantage for the importing country, but are still considered dumping in terms of national anti-dumping procedures.[30] The ultimate cause of the distortion in competition, namely the monopoly or cartel in the market of the exporting country creating a disadvantage to the exporting country through differential price-setting, is not included in the analysis of the anti-dumping procedures, however. An abuse supervisory authority able to cross borders would make this possible. The competition authorities of the exporting country would have to break up, or at least control, the monopoly or cartel in a case of market position dumping and price differentiation.

From a competition policy perspective, replacing national anti-dumping procedures with an international, abuse supervisory authority would be the best solution. This would probably encounter considerable resistance from national industries, however, since the dumping cases that would then no longer be considered – for example, getting rid of over-production at below-cost prices in a foreign country – would run counter to their interests. According to a study conducted by the OECD, only 28 out of 282 US anti-dumping proceedings between 1979 and 1989 met the criterion of a market-dominating position.[31] In addition, an important protectionist instrument would disappear with the national anti-dumping procedures.

Abuse supervisory authority at the international level

The abuse supervisory authority is a very inexact competition policy instrument owing to the difficulties in determining the relevant market and the position of the company in this market, but for lack of better options we cannot do without it. The analytic difficulties in ascertaining the market and the relative position are surmountable even with the two imprecise variables,[32] but it may be assumed to be even more difficult on the international level to set the criteria for an abuse of a market-dominating position owing to culture differences and the expected lobbying influence. One task of an international system of competition regulations would thus be to prevent the abuse of market-dominating positions on the international level, and another would be to create legal clarity with a unified framework for the abuse supervisory authority and to prevent the abuse of these instruments as a protectionist device.

There is a very great need for harmonization, since markets are internationally very different in more ways than their distinctive geographical features alone, and their use of the abuse controls varies greatly. A decentralized application of the abuse principle should therefore be carried out through national competition authorities. The international coordination of the abuse controls would have to make sure that the markets are defined and controlled across boundaries. An after-the-fact harmonization within the given competition policy framework could be undertaken by an international reference authority, which would establish the unified interpretation of an international abuse supervisory authority without a real loss of sovereignty. This does not apply to the necessary after-the-fact coordination of competition policies against international abuses from the national authorities. An intrusion upon national sovereignty from an international competition authority is in this case unavoidable. This task cannot be fulfilled by a court, since a court does not sit in permanent session and is therefore unable continuously to coordinate or direct the international competition policy procedures of several national competition authorities.

Vertical relationships

A vertical relationship is an agreement between producers or between producers and retailers at different production levels. Examples would be price assurances (content assurances) and production restrictions, exclusivity assurances and linking agreements (business assurances).[33] This type of market access restriction has become well known through the Japanese *keiretsu* system. Many markets are protected with exclusivity assurances in Japan. Retailers and producers are dependent on one another. These relationships are partially assured by familial connections. Competition exists only between the keiretsus.[34]

Vertical agreements of any kind are a hindrance to both domestic and international competition, yet they may also represent an advantage in terms of efficiency. Any advantages in efficiency are rarely passed on to consumers, however. There are many authors who see vertical relationships as a necessary evil, and even attribute positive effects to them:

1. The Chicago School argues that were exclusivity assurances between producers and retailers to disappear, both would have to set a profit margin, which in turn would mean a higher price for the consumer than the exclusive price set by the producer.[35]
2. The most relevant argument for the positive net welfare effects of vertical relationships is that the creation of monopolies in a certain field makes it possible to finance an extensive service and business network.
3. A third and final argument is that without an exclusive market agreement, the retailers would not be able to afford the market development costs, such as marketing expenses. Without such an agreement, they could be squeezed out of the market by another retailer who could undercut their prices by being a free-rider and avoiding the market development costs.[36] Vertical agreement could therefore strengthen competition against other producers in some cases.[37]

The first argument is easy to disprove. If one assumes that producers operate according to profit maximization, the monopolist producer will set prices on the foreign market dependent upon the demand elasticity to be found there, and offer the retailer a share of the item profits. In free international competition, the prices cannot be differentiated since there would be an arbitrage, as exports would otherwise go from the low-priced country to the high-priced one. This is the reason for the use of exclusivity to enforce resale price maintenance. The final sale price would be lower without them. The argument of the Chicago School, that the consideration of efficiency must take precedence in the producer's attempts at vertical concentrations, since a price increase in production and service automatically reduces the demand for the product, applies only for a price-elastic demand. That would support competition policy judgement of vertical price assurances through the national competition authorities. They could analyse the individual cases, in order to be able to differentiate according to the relative price elasticity.[38]

The second argument is validated by interviews with car dealers conducted by the author. Exclusivity assurances are standard in the auto industry. The dealers commit themselves to a market, train their employees in the corresponding auto types, and stock their replacement parts. They attempt to establish their brand regionally on the market and create a customer loyalty. In this case, vertical exclusivity assurances lead to a reduction in transaction, information and repair costs for dealers through specialization, which in turn can be passed on to the customer as long as competition is prevalent. In return, they demand regional protection, so that another supplier, without the service obligations, cannot undercut them in cost. For the dealer, it is decisively important that what the producer supplies is so comprehensive that all the requirements of the customer can be met. This means that the producer must have a broad enough palette of products and the necessary logistics to be able to break into a foreign market. The biggest market entrance barrier is these fixed costs.[39]

The manufacturer can use the brand monopoly to implement their own price and market policy. Intra-brand price competition is expressly prohibited. If the manufacturer is successful in differentiating their product from others in this way, they have attained a nearly perfect monopoly, with which they can maximize their profits through market divisions and price differentiation at the cost of the consumer.[40] Exactly because vertical relationships often lead to the sealing off of national markets and thus go against the EU-domestic market principle, the EU prohibition principle applies to vertical restrictions on competition as well as horizontal ones (EC Treaty, art. 81).[41]

The third argument needs to be differentiated. It applies only for high market development costs that do not automatically lead to a consumer relationship with the retailer. A time limit on the exclusivity agreements based on the example of patent protection would contribute more to overall welfare than an unlimited brand monopoly. It is all the better that meanwhile there is broad international consensus to prohibit at least the fixing of resale prices, even if there seems to be no possibility of prohibiting exclusivity agreements.[42]

In summary, whether vertical business relationships lead to restrictions on competition depends on whether or not competition with another substitutable product exists (inter-brand competition), and whether or not manufacturers use exclusivity agreements to create price differentiation. These variables could be investigated on an individual case basis. This is why vertical business relationships should be dealt with on the international level using the rules of reason; in other words, weighing the advantages and disadvantages for each case independently through a competition-regulating institution.[43] The approved vertical business relationships would then be placed under the supervision of an abuse supervisory authority.

Merger controls

Whereas a possible restriction on competition through power concentration is placed in the foreground for horizontal mergers, vertical mergers can restrict market access by way of easily coordinated behaviour and by denying the competition access to materials.[44] International mergers and takeovers have increased dramatically in the last few decades. The transaction volume of global mergers and takeovers was US$2.5 billion in 1998, five times that of the annual average in the early nineties.[45] There still are no coordinated international controls on mergers. A foreign merger can be reported to national competition authorities on the basis of the effects doctrine[46] if it has an effect on domestic competition, however.[47] The fusion controls applied by the national competition authorities are costly, time-consuming, and not calculable for international groups of companies, since they have to apply for approval in each country in which they are economically active, and thus have to deal with all the different legal systems.

In the case of international trade, this leads to multiple investigations of the same market position by different national competition authorities, since market power in foreign markets is always taken into consideration.[48] The Canadian aluminium producer ALCAN, the Swiss ALGROUP and the French company Pechiney would have had to register their merger in 40 countries, for example. They did so in 16.[49] Exaggerated merger requirements can arise when different national competition authorities demand the sale of various branches or subsidiaries even though a single sale would have brought about the desired reduction in market power.[50]

The goal of fusion controls is to prevent a market-dominating position from being either created or strengthened from which welfare-reducing restrictions on competition could be implemented.

The potential reduction in welfare from such reductions stands opposite the welfare gains that are to be had from size advantages such as economies of large scale or efficiency gains from savings on such institutions as personnel or research departments. In merger control, each case thus has to be looked at individually and the expected welfare gains and losses weighed. This is why an individual consideration based on the so-called rule of reason takes place in every national merger control process, regardless of whether it is undertaken by a competition authority or by a court.[51]

Although merger controls are not internationally taken for granted as a part of national competition regulatory systems, 40 countries implemented merger controls in 1998.[52] Notification is dealt with in various ways, however. In Canada, Germany, Ireland, New Zealand and the USA, only mergers that meet certain criteria have to be registered ahead of time. In Japan, all mergers have to be registered, while in France, registration is completely voluntary. There are also general differences internationally in application. Merger controls are less important in the USA than in the EU, for example, since the American courts currently give more weight to the efficiency gains from mergers owing to the influence of the Chicago School.[53]

In the practical application of merger prohibition, several problems present themselves. The insufficiencies of the criteria for intervention by the abuse supervisory authority in cases of market-dominating position are also found in cases of merger control, since there the same criteria for intervention apply. The size criterion seems arbitrary, since the relevant market is so difficult to determine conclusively. The fact that structural changes and branch specificities cannot be taken into consideration just adds to this factor. Since, as already explained, it is difficult to prove market domination, in cases of doubt courts tend to decide in favour of mergers.[54] Up to February 1998, the EU had prevented only eight mergers.[55] The effects of merger controls cannot be underestimated, however, since the notifiication regulations have already prevented many companies from competition-restricting mergers.

Economists also demand the international coordination at least of the merger controls. The suggested strategy is similar to the subsidiarity principle. The greater the international external effects of the merger, and the smaller the differences between the national concepts of competition policy, the more international the merger controls should be.[56] The Merger Task Force of the EU has been suggested as an example here, as it is used only for mergers that cross borders, and leaves all other merger controls to the national competition authorities of the member states.[57]

As with the abuse advisory authority, a decentralized use of the international merger controls through the national competition authorities is advisable to overcome the difficulties in application. A national authority can define the market more exactly owing to its closeness to it and thus better determine the market position. Because ever more mergers are taking place across borders, however, a decentralized merger control would have to be internationally coordinated with uniform criteria. Adopting a unified framework of action through the international community of states is a viable solution. In order not to complicate such an agreement any more than necessary, the criteria for action or intervention should remain as general as possible. There are no reasonable, binding, internationally valid criteria, owing to the different national market constellation. Specification of the criteria would take place in the decentralized application case by case by way of the national competition authorities.

An appeal authority could assure the coordinated application of the competition policy framework for mergers, much as with the abuse supervisory authority, but it would be unable to bring about the necessary cooperation across borders for the national competition authorities. The rule of reason seems a feasible competition policy solution, especially for international merger controls, making it possible to weigh, case for case, the positive externalities in the form of synergy effects against the negative welfare effects from the restriction on competition; this corresponds to the neo-ordoliberal concept that has been developed here.[58] An international authority is absolutely necessary, however. This is the one weakness of the current system of competition regulations, if one ignores the distortions to competition caused by national economic politics, which cannot be eliminated except with an intrusion upon national sovereignty. Regulation at the international level is absolutely necessary for the international coordination of merger controls and the abuse supervisory authority.[59] The intrusion upon national sovereignty can be kept to the minimum necessary for competition policy coordination, which would be the competence and assignment of the national competition authorities.

In summary, the many points of agreement in all important competition policy instruments – as shown by Subramanian – are to be considered very positive.[60] This realization contradicts the common assumption that national competition systems are too fundamentally different to allow international standardization.[61] It is true that an internationally recognized theory of competition does not yet exist, nor thus exact, detailed common guidelines, yet trends are visible, as this chapter has shown. International agreement exists, for example, on the damage caused by horizontal restrictions on competition, such as supply and price cartels, and subventions for exports. An international prohibition on such competition restrictions ought, therefore, meet with very little resistance.[62]

Requirements for an international competition authority

Several objections are made to an international institution for competition. First, it is said that an obligatory system of competition regulations would go against the foreign trade interests and definitions of sovereignty for several countries.[63] Second, some critics warn against transferring competition policy competence to a single supranational institution. They fear that this institution could become an uncontrollable, dictatorial central authority far removed from reality, which could make faulty decisions aimed at a conception of competition based on unclear theoretical guidelines.[64] Third, a uniform international codex of competition would, it is argued, prevent the most efficient system of competition between states.[65]

The first critique is of a general nature, and could also be used against the WTO as a super-ordinate, supranational authority in its field. Despite the justified scepticism, the progress towards trade liberalization within the GATT reached up this point should not be discounted, nor the fact that in 1947, with the ITO, an international competition authority was almost created, failing only because of the USA.[66] Who would have expected that the Uruguay Round would change the dispute settlement from unanimous acceptance of the panel proposals to a unanimous rejection? National competition laws are already being brought into line with each other in a liberal direction, and competition controls intensified.[67] There is also the intention to start negotiations about international rules for competition in the Doha Round. At the national level, there seems to be increasing acceptance of the inherent necessity for state controls on competition. The USA and the EU see themselves forced to bring their merger control mechanisms into line with one another, owing to the cross-border merger and takeover designs of their companies. The increased importance of the EU in world trade and its growing extraterritorial legal stance[68] demonstrates to the USA the advantage of an internationally harmonized merger authority. Since the USA cannot force its interests in the face of resistance from the EU, it will probably abandon its entrenched position, at least on the point of an international merger control.

The second critique should be taken seriously, but a dictatorial exercise of power can be prevented with appropriate controls on the international institution. The third point of critique can be refused by the competition policy problems in international trade that have been explained in this chapter. For one thing, competition between nations, and their companies, takes place within competition policy anarchy, owing to the prisoner's dilemma, at the cost of international welfare. The market mechanism thus fails at the international level. For another, there are inefficiencies above all in the international merger controls – as has been shown – owing to a lack of regulations. Arguments against the creation of an effective international system of competition regulations are far from convincing when seen in the light of the distortions of competition in international trade. Critics of such an international system generally agree on this point:

> Maybe the setting up of an international antitrust policy is the price for abolishing these anti-competitive and trade distorting trade policy instruments. If the focus was on eliminating these trade policy instruments, and if the implementation of an international antitrust policy was the complement to abolishing these measures, our evaluation would clearly be more positive.[69]

Designing a new international system for competition regulation

To set up an international competition policy, the international community of states has to decide on an international norm as a legislative body in the form of an international competition law or codex. A codex alone cannot guarantee a functional system of competition, however. An executive organ must implement the codex, with enough ways of sanctioning for it to be able to bring the behaviour of the market competitors into line with the rules.

A decentralized structure seems to be the best model for an international competition authority, as demonstrated previously. The national cartel authorities would be in charge of any international authority. The distribution of tasks should take place according to the principle of subsidiarities.[70] The authorities familiar with local and national circumstances should find it easier to reach a resolution for restrictions on competition contained within regional boundaries than would a far-removed super-ministry. In the case of international restrictions on competition, however, it would be the job of the international authority to coordinate the resolution and sanctions.

Up to this point, we have worked out two central elements for an international system for competition regulations: a legal system that establishes sanctions for deviations from the basic principles of free and equal competition, and a politically independent international competition authority that functions as an executive organ to implement and enforce the legal system. In order to avoid arbitrariness and mistakes on the part of this executive, a control and review authority is necessary in the form of an international court, before which complainants could bring a case against the decision of the executive. This would also prevent the problem of a dictatorial use of power. The determination of the legal system would also be the responsibility of the court. This international court of competition would be accessible to all parties affected in a case, including private parties.

In 1973, Germany founded an independent consultation and control authority, the monopoly commission, according to the second amendment to the Act Against Restrictions on Competition, in order to support the legislative and executive organs with a panel of experts, as well as to reduce the influence of interest groups. It is responsible for formulating an expert opinion on the competition policy of the Federal cartel authority and on the competition laws of the legislature.[71] Such an independent consulting and control authority needs to be established at the international level. This neutral scientific authority would comment on the decisions taken by the international competition authority and the international court of competition. Such a move would not only force the international competition authority to reflect upon an exclusively economically oriented, neutral third-party opinion, but would also increase the transparency of the decisions, and thus public acceptance of them as well. This new authority would be, above all, responsible for clearly articulating consumer interest in its opinions, thereby creating a political awareness, in order to help compensate for the organizational disadvantage of consumers at the international level.

The international competition authority would have to be supplied with enough staff with access to all the documents concerning national budgeting decisions. High membership dues, to be paid back five years later, could serve to secure the competition authority's ability to enforce its decisions upon resisting states without having to be authorized to impinge upon national sovereignty. If a country refused to comply with a decision of the competition authority, it could hold back payments or even cancel them. Were a country to refuse to pay the membership dues, it would be collectively shut out of the trade freedoms (most-preferred status) by the other states.

It is vital for the economic rationality of any decisions taken by these three institutions that political influence by governments is made impossible. The posts at the international competition authority should therefore be given according to the importance of each member country at the lower levels, although the authority should decide for itself who best fits the requirements for the leading positions. The deciding council of the international competition authority must be made up of experts who have distinguished themselves both in economic science and in practical expertise. Dismissals from office for clearly wrong behaviour would be left to the international court of competition. To keep the decisions of the international court of trade independent from political influence, the judges would be appointed for life. National states would be allowed to suggest multiple candidates. The actual choice should be left to the international court of competition, however, after its initial composition, in order to maintain a high-quality group of neutral and objective judges.

4

Strategies to Reform the Regulations on International Competition

Having worked out our economic ideal competition order, this chapter summarizes the general discussion on reform and makes several reform suggestions. The first part comprises an explanation of the criteria by which to evaluate reform suggestions, while the second presents, compares and evaluates a selection of the most important suggestions. The third part brings everything together in conclusion.

Criteria for an international system to regulate competition

The requirements for an international regulatory system for competition are different from those for national economic regulations in one fundamental way; namely, in the actors involved. Firms compete both nationally and internationally, whereas sovereign states compete on the global level for their share of international value creation. States try to maximize their profits, just as individuals do. They represent the interests of their firms as international actors and try to maximize their affluence and growth by way of their national economic policy, even if foreign countries sometimes have to take the brunt. International regulations have the task of establishing a framework in such a way that the benefit maximizations of the private firms and governments lead to a globally maximized affluence; in other words, the 'invisible hand' of international competition is allowed to develop. According to our neo-ordoliberal approach, international resources must be directed towards the most efficient production possible and all of the potential in competition developed, so that both national and global affluence can be maximized.

One often hears demands for fair international competition. Competition should indeed make the effort to be fair, since a regulatory system that is felt to result in unfair distribution will not be accepted. Above all, a system will be fair when the implementing institutions can resist providing any one-sided bias or subjectivity. This can be accomplished by way of an independent person, a mediating party or a court. Transparency and an easily understandable verdict are another two requirements necessary for the acceptance of a decision.

We have now identified two criteria for an international competition regulatory system. The first is increasing international welfare by guaranteeing international production efficiency and freedom of competition as the basis for the development of competition's functions. Restrictions on competition must be weighed against the effects of an economic policy intervention in the market. The rules of productive competition must be enforced (see Chapter 1 for the rules that must be followed). The second criterion is the acceptance of the system itself. These two goals represent the increased advantage, or 'returns', of such a regulatory system. A prioritized list of preferences for the current reform strategies can be created just as it is for a consumer good according to net profit – that is to say, the difference between net profit and net loss or the advantage minus the disadvantage (the Kaldor–Hicks criterion; see also Chapter 1).

In order for the advantages to be realized, the relationship of the goals to each other must be analysed. They are independent of one another, since the goal of increasing international productivity does not hinder the goal of acceptance for the regulations and vice versa. Maximizing these two goals is a secondary target of international advantage maximization; in other words, global affluence. Implementing the regulations is a constant challenge as well. For an international competition system this is the challenge of the organizational and political expense of implementation, which can be observed in the political resistance that must be overcome in order to realize a system of controls. In general one can assume that the resistance will be directly proportional to the level of interference with national sovereignty. The loss of sovereignty can be calculated as a loss of freedom when one weighs one's advantages. In the end, however, we can reach only a qualitative prioritized list of preferences, since advantages can only be classified cardinally, not ordinally.

Table 4.1 represents visually the various strategies of reform and their individual qualities. In Table 4.2 they are put in order of their comparative advantage according to the criteria worked out, which are applied in the following pages. In Table 4.2 the evaluation is based on a scale of −5 to +5, whereas the criteria 'organizational expense' and 'acceptance' are given less importance with the weighted value 0.5, since we are dealing here with mostly short-term expenditures or losses in the implementation phase of the new competition regulatory system. The continued gains in affluence resulting from increased international efficiency in production and the productive development of competition contribute to the advantages, with a weight of 2.

The evaluation of the strategies is indeed subjective to a certain degree, owing to the unavoidable choice of criteria and weighted values. The value of the analyses is therefore in the differentiated evaluation itself, and not so much in the results of the evaluation or the ratings. It is thus left to the reader to adjust the weights on the basis of the given analysis and come to their own respective results.

Evaluation of selected reform strategies

Giardina and Beviglia-Zampetti propose establishing an international court for international trade conflicts, which could function as an extension of the current WTO system by allowing private entities to have access as well.[1] Matoo and Subramanian also plead for the international coordination of national competition policy within the framework of a conflict resolution process. An international agreement would provide the basis for such a process, in that the countries would be obliged to make their national competition authorities and courts accessible to all parties, including foreign companies and consumers. The authorities should provide independent consumer representation, however, since the organizational difficulties and transaction costs for consumers are prohibitively high. An international agreement would also make national competition authorities and their respective governments responsible for providing to foreign authorities the information necessary for the implementation of the competition procedure. An organ of conflict resolution would be available to all parties to a dispute, and would guarantee the execution

Table 4.1 Strategy for reform

Strategy[1]	*Special characteristics on the internalization of negative external effects*	*Instruments of competition policy*					*Institutions*			
		Horizontal agreements	*Vertical agreements (restrictions on competition)*	*Abuses*	*Mergers*	*Comity P: Positive N: Negative*	*International court*	*Measures for redress from the exporting country*	*International competition authorities (a) Decentralized coordination of the national authorities*	*International competition authorities (b) Central control over the national authorities*
1. Giardina and Beviglia-Zampetti (GBZ)[2]	Traffic-light-strategy for restrictions on competition; common consensus in connection with case-law strategy			To be determined			X	Implicit	Distribution of responsibilities	
2. Matoo and Subramanian[3]	Common consensus, imposition of consumer interests, equality for all parties before national competition authorities, information required of the national competition authorities			To be determined			X	Explicit; independent representation of consumer interests		
3. Hauser and Schoene[4]	Effects doctrine (ED) and cooperation agreement	ED	ED	ED	–		X	Implicit		
4. ABA-Report[5]	Only for export cartels	Prohibition of export cartels			Harmonization from below	P				

5. Fox and Ordover[6]	Cooperation agreement and set of competition rules, global welfare, decentralized competition policy through accessibility of the national legal systems	Prohibition	–	Only restrictions prohibited, and replacement of anti-dumping measures	Controls	N	X	–	–	
6. Van Miert Strategy[7]	Long-term: principle of prohibition for horizontal and vertical restrictions on competition, rules of reason-strategy	Prohibition/ Rule of reason	Rule of reason	Prohibition	Harmonization from below	P N	X	Implicit	Long-term	Necessary
7. DIAC[8]	Principle of prohibition for horizontal and vertical restrictions on competition on domestic trade, international process initiation, decentralized competition policy by way of equal access to national legal systems	Prohibition/ Rule of reason	Prohibition/ Rule of reason	Prohibition	Controls		X	Implicit	X	–
8. Scherer[9]	Obligatory information from national competition authorities	Prohibition of import and export cartels		Prohibition	Controls		X	Explicit	X	Medium-term

[1] Ordered according to loss of sovereignty. See the cited literature for further details on the strategies themselves.
[2] See Giardina and Zampetti (1997).
[3] See Mattoo and Subramanian (1997).
[4] See Hauser and Schoene (1994).
[5] See OECD (1994b).
[6] See Fox and Ordover (1995).
[7] See EU Commission (ed.) (1995).
[8] See Fikentscher and Immenga (1995).
[9] See Scherer (1994).

Table 4.2 Rating of the reform strategies

Strategy[1]	*Loss of sovereignty*	*Organizational expense*	*Disadvantages*	*Increase in allocation efficiency*	*Acceptance*	*Advantages*	*Net advantage*
Column:	1	2	Σ1, 2	4	5	Σ4, 5	Σ1, 2, 4, 5
Weight:	1	0.5		2	0.5		
1. GBZ[2]	+4	+5	+6.5	+1	−2	0	+6.5
2. Matoo and Subramanian	+4	+5	+6.5	+1	−3	+0.5	+7
3. Hauser and Schoene	+4	+5	+6.5	+0.5	−5	−1.5	+8
4. ABA-Report	+5	+5	+7.5	+0.5	0	+1	+8.5
5. Fox and Ordover	+4	+4	+6	+2	+1	4.5	+10.5
6. Van Miert Strategy	+5	+4	+7	+3	+2	+7	+14.5
7. IAC	+3	+3	+4.5	+4	+3	+9.5	+14
8. Scherer	−5	−5	−7.5	+5	+3	+10.5	+18

[1] Ordered according to loss of sovereignty; graph of my own construction and that of Wins (2000), p. 139.
[2] Giardina and Beviglia-Zampetti.

of the international common denominator in agreed rules on competition, such as already exist to a limited extent in the GATT (equal rights in competition courts, for example, and equal market access). This would be achieved by empowering the complainants to implement reactive measures.[2]

The organizational expense (+3) of the implementation suggested by Giardina and Beviglia-Zampetti and the loss of sovereignty (+4) are both low, since neither a harmonization of the national competition authorities nor the creation of an international authority is prescribed; they rely on the existing WTO dispute resolution mechanisms. The same applies to the suggestion put forth by Matoo and Subramanian as well as that of Hauser and Schoene.

The strategy developed by Hauser and Schoene is based exclusively on the effects doctrine. Hauser and Schoene suggest an international agreement as the means to implement the effects doctrine, as do many other authors. Such an agreement would both provide for the creation of a dispute settlement tribunal and make it possible to force national anti-trust authorities to turn over information to foreign exporters.[3] Sanctions from foreign authorities would be legitimate in the case of uncooperative national antitrust authorities opposing restrictions on domestic competition, and would place all foreign companies at a disadvantage.

At first glance, the effects doctrine seems to be the ideal solution. It eliminates the need to create a new law on competition, which circumvents the need for member states to reach an agreement on anything new. Tedious negotiations and the unavoidable necessity of making compromises on competition policy would thus be avoided and the international acceptance of such a solution would probably be quite high. Competition between international regulatory systems to find the best solution would also remain effective.[4] All external effects on competition could be taken into consideration, were all countries to apply the effects doctrine, as the competition authorities can use their national competition laws against all possible restrictions on competition – while having an impact on their domestic market independent of the location of the enterprises that caused it.

This positive impression does not pass closer inspection, however. The effects of competition on foreign competitors would indeed be dealt with were the effects doctrine systematically applied, but intervention in competition policy does not take place in the country of origin. This is similar to the anti-dumping measures in a foreign country, where the effects – but not the causes – of restrictions on competition in the land of origin are addressed.[5] In addition, only the direct effects of competition are taken into account. The domestic effects that have no direct effect on the supply abroad but hamper access to foreign markets because of their restrictions on domestic competition are not considered.

The effects doctrine can also be criticized for involving only domestic competition policy. The controlling market position of a domestic company on a foreign market, for example, is not addressed.[6] It is also imaginable for the competitive behaviour of a foreign company to be in breach of the domestic country's rules on competition, but to be acceptable under international law. The domestic competition authorities would use the effects doctrine on a legal basis that was inapplicable in the home country of the exporter. A very high potential for conflict would be created by this situation. The objective implementation of the doctrine would also be questionable, not only because the foreign company could put pressure on its government to provide support, since it can be assumed that the rules would be applied less stringently to domestic companies,[7] but also, above all, because the opportunity for the national governments to enforce their domestic laws on foreign companies could lead to the national rules being used in a protectionist sense, just like national anti-dumping measures.[8] Klodt has researched the most pertinent applications of the effects doctrine with regard to whether they could be the source of international conflict that could, in turn, be solved by cooperation between national competition authorities based on positive comity. He came to the conclusion that out of 22 cases an effective cooperation took place in 5 and would have solved the problem in 2 others. On the other hand, cooperation failed in 8 cases because the violations took place in the country that was applying the effects doctrine, and in 7 further cases the cooperation failed because of diverging industrial policy goals (see Table 4.3). The industrial policy goals were directed towards the aim of strengthening the position of each country's own industry at the cost of other countries, which amounts to a restriction to competition initiated by the state. Klodt then concludes that an intensification of the cooperation between national competition authorities is not developed enough to tackle cross-border competition violations.[9] This illustrates again the need for an international authority to prevent abuses of national competition rules, which Hauser and Schoene, in fact, admit.[10]

The effects doctrine would be a workable alternative to national anti-dumping measures. Since proof of a distortion in competition in the country of the exporter is required for an intervention under the doctrine, its use would be limited to dumping cases where the foreign manufacturer had a monopoly or was a member of a price cartel in the exporting country. On the other hand, it is not impossible that the national competition authorities might use the doctrine as a protectionist instrument. Last but not least, problems remain with regard to the enforcement of domestic competition rules on foreign companies, and the ineffectiveness of domestic competition authorities due to the lack of an independent enforcement authority when proof is sought of restrictions on competition caused from abroad.

For the reasons mentioned above, the strategy of Hauser and Schoene does not go far in eliminating restrictions on international competition (+0.5), whereas the other two attempts at a strategy consider a code of competition to be a minimal requirement of consensus (+1). Following the successes of the 'traffic light strategy',[11] including the formulation of an internationally acceptable agreement on the issue of subsidies, Giardina and Beviglia-Zampetti suggest dividing competition violations into red (strictly forbidden), yellow (situational yet prosecutable) and green (allowed and thus not prosecutable). This idea was evaluated positively and deserves to be discussed on the international level. A symbolic differentiation divides restrictions into more manageable categories, allowing them to be more efficiently addressed. The idea from Matoo and Subramanian[12] of making a procedure accessible for all involved parties, including foreign companies and private parties, bodes success because the authorities and courts can make more objective decisions when they are able to take the interests of all sides into consideration. The idea of taking consumer interests into consideration through national involvement is also a good suggestion for enhancing wealth (see the interdependences presented above in the goals of competition policy), though establishing independent interest representation would be even more appropriate. Despite the positive arguments, however, most violations of competition would fail to be resolved by this suggestion.

All three strategies are based mostly on an international competition policy mediation process. The international harmonizing and

Table 4.3 Selected examples of the effects doctrine

Decision, year	*Decision-making body*	*Substance of the decision*	*Solved through cooperation*	*Solvable through cooperation*	*Competitive national norms*	*Competitive industrial policies*
1. Alcoa, 1945	US Supreme Court	First application of the effects doctrine based on the Sherman Acts against a quota cartel in Switzerland closed to the US market.			×	
2. Ciba/Geigy, 1970	US Department of Justice	Market behaviour for the fusion of two Swiss companies that was acceptable according to Swiss law, but not US law.			×	
3. Tar Color, 1972	ECJ	An export cartel that was illegal in the EU as target country but was legal for the US producers involved under US law.			×	
4. Organic Pigments, 1979	German BGH	BGH adhered to the statutory obligation to report two merging US companies in Germany.		×		
5. Bayer/ Firestone, 1980	Supreme Court, Berlin	The Federal Cartel Office enforced the prohibition of two French branches of multinational companies against the industrial policy of France in the German Supreme Court.				×

6. Uranium, 1981	US Federal Trade Commission	A decision of the US of the authorities against a price cartel from foreign companies on the US market was stopped by the governments of Great Britain, Canada, South Africa, Australia and France.	×	
7. Philip Morris/ Rothmans, 1983	Supreme Court, Berlin	The Federal Cartel Office forbade the merger of a South African company with an American one that had already been approved. The merger took place under the condition that Rothmans separate from a German subsidiary.		×
8. IBM, 1985	US Department of Justice	The EU tried in vain to force IBM to announce new product standards for Europe, so that the European producers could develop their own products in time. The goal was to prevent the expansion of IBM into the European periphery market. The US Department of Justice rejected it because of strong competition in the USA.		×

Table 4.3 Continued

Decision, year	*Decision-making body*	*Substance of the decision*	*Solved through cooperation*	*Solvable through cooperation*	*Competitive national norms*	*Competitive industrial policies*
9. Laker Airways, 1985	US Federal Trade Commission	After the bankruptcy of the British airline Laker, the bankruptcy administrator sued other airlines in American courts for predatory pricing. The US courts declared it their jurisdiction because American airlines were also affected. The British government forbade the administrator to provide the court with documents of proof, since predatory pricing is not forbidden in Great Britain.			×	
10. Cellulose, 1988	ECJ	Affirmation of the EU Commission's decision to prohibit an export cartel for cellulose, which was based exclusively in third countries.			×	
11. Mérieux/ Connaught, 1990	US Federal Trade Commission	The US Federal Trade Commission imposed conditions on the merger of a Canadian and a French company without consulting either government. They were then included after a massive protest.			×	

12. De Havilland/ ATR, 1993	EU Commission	The merger of a Canadian and a French company was prohibited by the EU Commission, even though Canada and the USA supported it.			×
13. Hartford Fire Insurance, 1993	US Supreme Court	The US Supreme Court forbade British reinsurance certain contracts that were allowed under British law but not under US law (despite comity agreements between the EU and USA).		×	
14. Fax paper, 1994	Canadian Bureau of Competition Policy/US Department of Justice	A cross-border price cartel was discovered through much cooperation between US American and Canadian competition authorities. Each authority supported the efforts at discovery from the other side.	×		
15. Plastic tableware, 1994	Canadian Bureau of Competition Policy/US Department of Justice	A cross-border price cartel was discovered through much cooperation between US American and Canadian competition authorities. Each authority supported the efforts at discovery from the other side.	×		
16. British, Telecom/MCI, 1995	EU Commission	Successful cooperation between US American and European competition authorities that	×		

Table 4.3 Continued

Decision, year	*Decision-making body*	*Substance of the decision*	*Solved through cooperation*	*Solvable through cooperation*	*Competitive national norms*	*Competitive industrial policies*
		led to the prohibition of a British–US area cartel.				
17. Kimberley Clark/ Scott Paper, 1996	EU Commission	Successful cooperation between US American and European competition authorities that led to the prohibition of a merger of two US American companies.	×			
18. British Airways/ American Airlines, 1996	US Department of Transportation	Attempt by the US Department of Transportation to connect a strategic alliance between British Airways and American Airlines that had the approval of the British government with a general opening of London (Heathrow) Airport (despite a comity agreement between the EU and the USA).				×
19. Boeing/ McDonnell Douglas, 1997	EU Commission	The US Federal Trade Commission approved a merger between Boeing and McDonnell Douglas, even though the market-dominating position of Boeing would be strengthened both in				×

		the USA and in Europe, most likely to strengthen Boeing's position against the European Airbus industry. The EU Commission declined to forbid the merger or demand a 10% fine, and was satisfied with smaller conditions (for example, Boeing had to forgo an exclusive contract with Delta Airlines and American Airlines), in order to avoid a Transatlantic row (extraterritorial application of EU law despite a comity agreement between the EU and USA). The EU Commission refrained from an extraterritorial application, despite the negative comity of nations, not the least of which was due to the threat of trade policy sanctions from the USA.		
20. Worldcom/ MCI, 1998	EU Commission/ US Department of Justice	Successful cooperation between US and European competition authorities for the merger of Worldcom and MCI. A result of the fusion would have been the increase of combined market share of internet access to 50%, which would have decreased	×	

Table 4.3 Continued

Decision, year	*Decision-making body*	*Substance of the decision*	*Solved through cooperation*	*Solvable through cooperation*	*Competitive national norms*	*Competitive industrial policies*
		competition in both regions. The EU Commission imposed the condition that MCI sell its internet business, and the US Department of Justice agreed.				
21. Air Liquide/ BOC, 2000	US Federal Trade Commission	Approval of the merger between French and British industrial gas producing companies by the EU Commission despite a market-dominating position. The merger was prohibited by the US Federal Trade Commission (despite a comity agreement).				×
22. GE/Honeywell, 2001	EU Commission	The EU Commission forbade the merger between GE and Honeywell that had already been approved by US authorities (despite a comity agreement).			×	

Source: Klodt (2003), p. 46, p. 49, p. 54, p. 59, p. 60; Wins (2000), p. 3 and Without Author (2001), p. 13.

enforcement of policy principles through a mediation process has three main disadvantages. First, competition policy is not conducted at the level of a mediation court. Neither market supervision nor a control on mergers would result from mediation. The action of a mediating body on its own initiative is no more a part of the plan than controls on national economic policy for conformity of competition. Second, the enforcement of competition rules is dependent on the possibility for retaliation in the injured country. The private parties would be at the mercy of their governments. The list of Japanese–American conflicts in international trade compiled by Subramanian shows that the Japanese competition authorities complained about restrictions on competition only after the American government had come to the defence of its disadvantaged companies in Japan.[13] The EU and the USA would have a comparative advantage through this system because of the size of their economic zones, which allows them more imports and thus greater chances for redress. Third, it is very questionable whether, when applying domestic rules on foreign soil, the national government, especially the department responsible for competition, would cooperate with the foreign agency carrying out the mediation. Cooperating could, in fact, be against the interests of the domestic industry, and, because of the high transaction costs, a failure to cooperate would not automatically be brought before a mediation committee.

It can be assumed that the parties concerned would consider all three strategies to be fair because they include a mediating institution. The strategies that are concerned with only a minimally restrictive set of rules for competition, such as those of Giardina and Beviglia-Zampetti, and Matoo and Subramanian, allow for a low level of transparency and thus a low level of legal security as well (−3). Giardina and Beviglia-Zampetti do aim for a self-expanding case law, however (−2). The strategy of Hauser and Schoene offers no transparency or legal security, though, owing to the complete absence of international rules of competition (−5).

The special committee of the US Bar Association supports a 'harmonization' of national competition authorities from below in the form of a 'trial-and-error' process. The bottom-up approach assumes that national competition regulations will automatically harmonize through international political and economic interaction. The international competition agreement that is considered to be essential should be adopted when an undefined level of harmonization has been achieved. The two basic suggestions for improvement on the part of the US Bar Association,[14] namely the prohibition of export cartels within the framework of a multinational agreement, and international unification and increased cooperation for cross-border mergers, rate well as regards loss of sovereignty and organizational expense. This is owing to the principle of harmonization from the bottom up (+5). The advantage for the international community is extremely low, however, owing to the lack of obligation on states. Only an internationally binding agreement for export cartels is to be drawn up. In addition, the plan calls for an effective decentralized international competition policy by way of a bilateral competition agreement based on positive comity.

Until the cooperation agreement between the USA and the EU in 1991, only the term negative comity[15] was widely familiar. According to negative comity, a state should respect the interests of other states when applying its rules; that is to say, in international conflicts a state should refrain from extraterritorial application of their rules according to the effects doctrine if this contradicts the interests of a foreign state.[16] The USA–EU agreement expanded the rights of the state affected by restrictions on competition, by giving the right to the foreign country to demand that the state imposing the restriction apply its national rules in order to assert the foreign interests (positive comity).[17] Seen in this way, the positive comity principle would be capable of dealing with obstructions to international competition clearly originating from one country by way of the market knowledge and extensive competencies of the national competition authorities. National influence over competition would remain intact with a decentralized competition policy by way of bilateral agreements between state authorities, and national sovereignty would not be impinged upon by a control mechanism on national policy. In addition, the makeups of competition regulations in many countries are equivalent in enough ways for them to represent a realistic first step on the way to international regulations.

Despite positive comity, none of the bilateral agreements are compulsory, nor have they provided any enforceable legal claim on foreign application of law, not even on legal or official help in gathering information. The bilateral agreements relate only to the relationship between the authorities; competition courts are excluded from cooperation. The information given by the foreign authorities to the investigating domestic authorities is seriously restricted owing to continuing secrecy. Neither restrictions resulting from a governmental policy, nor restrictions covered by the rules of the country required to cooperate as in the example of cartels, can be addressed.[18] Mutual understanding is the basis of the cooperation agreement, because of the avoidance of limiting national sovereignty in any way; bilateral agreements do not go far enough for the reform of the international regulations.

Uninvolved countries are discriminated against by bilateral agreements, since they do not receive any preferential treatment. The economically stronger countries can systematically force their interests on a weaker country,[19] which destroys free trade as a collective good in the form of unrestricted market access. This shows that the GATT principles cannot be realized without support from competition policy. The further disadvantages of a decentralized competition policy are the absence both of homogenous and transparent requirements for competition and of instruments for international conflict resolution or mediation. An international merger and state aid control are also absent, as is a substitute for the international anti-dumping measures in the form of international abuse supervision to control market domination positions.[20] Many bilateral agreements also run contrary to the principle of most-preferred-nation status under the GATT. Besides the creation of groups, there is also a danger that the only countries to agree on regulations will be those with the economic clout to push through the interests of their industry and have the necessary administration. The consideration of the political interests of other countries in the context of positive and negative comity not only assumes goodwill on the part of the national authorities, but is hardly practical owing to the sheer numbers of countries that would have to be considered in calculating impacts.

There is no legal security, because the suggestions for improvement from the US Bar Association do not include international rules for competition. An international court is not provided for, which is why not much would change from the current anarchical regulations (+0.5), and the suggestions would hardly increase international acceptance (0).

Four years after the American Bar Association published its suggestion, the spokesman for the group, Fox,[21] published a much further developed strategy together with Ordover.[22] The goal of this competition policy strategy is the maximization of global welfare, defined by its authors as 'the aggregate level of consumers' benefits and profits realized by consumers and firms in all pertinent countries.[23] The starting-point for such an international system is the national competition regulations with their respective authorities and courts, which under a treaty would be obliged to cooperate with one another. In line with a narrow interpretation of negative comity, the national authorities would give equal weight to both the domestic and foreign effects of their decisions. All states party to the treaty would have equal access to the national law institutions. Cartels would be forbidden on principle, and vertical restrictions to competition would fall under the restriction abuse supervisory authority, which would generally guarantee that domestic market-dominating positions would be unable to restrict market access. A unified registration service for mergers would need to be developed. Mergers with international influence would have to be registered with an international registrar and the respective national competition authorities would then be informed. In general, all national policies with external effects, especially subventions, would have to published and justified annually by each signatory state. Since anti-dumping measures restrict foreign competition and/or market access, they would be replaced with a domestic abuse supervisory authority. A dispute settlement process would be created to address international conflicts.[24]

The approach of Fox and Ordover must be examined rather differently. Even though it does not require the creation of an international competition authority (+4) and leaves national sovereignty intact (+4), it includes far-reaching competition policy rules. These are compulsory only for horizontal restrictions (prohibitions) and vertical restrictions (obstruction abuse supervision) such as in the case of dumping within national competition rules. International coordination does not exist any more than does direct control over the national competition authorities, which is why neither a real reduction in the disruptions to competition, nor with it an increase in international allocation efficiency and productive freedom of competition, can be expected (+2). A step in the right direction would be the accessibility of the national legal systems for all of the signatory states of the proposed international competition agreement. It cannot be assumed, however, that the national authorities would take the interests of foreign states or their firms into consideration in the context of negative comity. Up to now, the experience of competition policy cooperation agreements has, in fact, shown the opposite. For the reasons stated above, a high acceptance level of this strategy cannot be expected, despite the proposed mediation measures (+1). The legal security is not to be taken for granted, either, owing to the lack of coordination on national competition policy decisions. Both the impingement on sovereignty and the organizational expense are low because of the decentralized nature of the transactions concerning competition policy, but can be rated higher than for the previous strategies (+4).

The EU and its high commissioner for competition, Van Miert, also saw an immediate need for action in competition policy at the international level. In 1994, Van Miert charged three internal and three external experts[25] with the task of creating a plan for an international system of competition regulations.[26] The European Van Miert reform strategy can be situated somewhere between what is realistic in the current political climate and the ideal rules of competition according to competition theory. It begins with bilateral cooperation on the basis of a positive and negative comity that is to flow over the long term into an international coordinating authority without intervention rights. The EU expert group adds that an international authority is necessary with its own autonomous competition policy and the power to intervene and impose sanctions. The experts also predict that the policy cooperation between national authorities on the basis of positive comity and an extended negative comity will succeed only if the competition authorities are independently aware of foreign interests as well as their own domestic tasks. In this way, the negative effects of the states could be counteracted from within their own areas of competence. As previously stated, non-compulsory bilateral agreements are not enough for an effective international control on competition. The EU expert group therefore sees the successive creation of a multilateral agreement with minimum standards as the long-term solution. Experience would indicate, however, that the further development of the competition policy would get stuck at the level of non-compulsory cooperation agreement.[27] The likelihood is very high that interest groups on the subject of anti-dumping such as in the USA and the EU would spring into being, which would lead to a segmentation of the international competition rules.

Keeping in mind that the EU group of experts would prefer an international authority to be allocated the competence of implementation, such a solution would be realizable only in the distant future because of the necessary and extensive harmonization and coordination of interests that it would require. For the suggested authorities without their own implementation abilities, no sovereignty would have to be compromised (+5). The organizational expense is also low (+4). A minimal competition code of rules that includes a prohibition on export cartels and, for all other restrictions, applies the rules of reason in conjunction with a mediating body does, in fact, offer only a minimum of legal security and transparency (+2) and a minimum of allocation efficiency and productive development of competition (+3). At least an abuse commission is provided for in principle. The disruptions in competition and the lack of legal security created by the different and sometimes protectionist ways of managing the national anti-dumping measures remain, just as does the disruption from uncoordinated merger controls. It is unclear to what extent the proposed international institution can assert itself with its non-binding proposals in the realization and further development of the minimum code of rules. The suggestion of expanding the non-violation dispute settlement mechanism in Article XXIII of the GATT to market access restrictions, and thus putting national economic policy under the control of international competition policy, is definitely to be considered positive. The same goes for the proposed use of the rules of reason for vertical restrictions. All in all, the national competition policies remain uncoordinated under the strategy of Van Miert.

The Draft International Anti-trust Code (DIAC)[28] was created by Immenga (among others), which is why there are similarities to the Van Miert suggestion. An important difference is that the DIAC provides for national authorities to be brought before a national court by the international authorities, should they fail to implement the international rules of competition. The international rules would be enforced by the International Anti-trust Authority (IAA), which has the authority to force states to enter proceedings and to substantiate their decisions by way of an international panel. If a state does not comply with the findings of the IAA, it can be brought before the responsible national court. The execution of competition policy remains the domain of the states themselves, however. Because of the ability of private parties to raise a legal complaint provided for in this proposal, the international authority is given control of national decisions and the panel is given the role of judge. It can be assumed that the international rules of competition will be more effectively implemented, since independent judges are more objective in their pronouncements than are the authorities that answer to governments. Access to the national courts is also granted to all interested parties, including foreign companies and private individuals.

Because the implementation of competition policy remains at the national level and the code within the framework of Article IV of the GATT applies only to states that want to sign, the loss of national sovereignty (+3) and the organizational expense (+3) may be higher than for the Van Miert suggestion, but they are still low. It may be difficult for the IAA in cases of international restrictions involving several countries to address each unfulfilled obligation. The proposed international minimum standards for the horizontal restrictions on competition are identical with those for the long-term, according to Van Miert. The DIAC goes another step further with vertical restrictions and proposes a principle of prohibition *per se* within the framework of the rules of reason. The international mergers tolerated by Van Miert would here be placed under an international control that could go so far as to break them up.

The assumption of the DIAC that every state has a national competition authority is not true and has indeed been criticized. This critique applies, in fact, to all of the strategies that are based on a decentralized international competition policy. On the other hand, the conception of the DIAC by no means envisions all states immediately signing such a set of rules – quite the opposite: it can be assumed that the existence of such a code would be a motive to create competition authorities in accordance with the rules. In addition, the DIAC has been accused of being too concentrated on anti-trust policies. The national anti-dumping laws are not to be integrated into the DIAC, but rather will continue to exist with all of their faults. In the same way, an abuse commission is provided for, but no suggestions for a workable definition for such slippery terms as 'market power' or 'relevant market' are given.[29] It is also debatable whether states would subject themselves to an international panel within the framework of the DIAC and, for that matter, if the international community would ever be able to agree on an enforceable set of rules that could eventually lead to the breakup of their powerful companies.[30] The DIAC does not provide any help in a situation in which a national competition authority refuses to take measures against a restriction by way of a domestic company and the national court – in which the IAA has raised the complaint – covers up the inaction, causing it to be in violation of the international court's judgement. In the end, control over national policy gets left out, and hence many disruptions to international competition will continue. Only on this point does the Van Miert strategy go further, in that it expands the

GATT non-violation dispute to cover the effects of competition on national policy.

The DIAC represents a compromise that combines a meaningful reduction in competition disruptions with a decentralized political realization (+4). The legal security and transparency, and thus the acceptance that can be reasonably expected, are rated higher than for the previous strategies (+3) because of the comprehensive and strict rules of competition and the verifiability facilitated by access to the national courts for all parties concerned.

The strategy proposed by Scherer[31] is doubtless the one to address most effectively the necessary international coordination of the national competition policies. An international competition policy office (ICPO) intervenes directly in the national policy and proscribes actions to be undertaken to increase international coordination when restrictions arise. A binding set of international rules is also included. Both import and export cartels are prohibited. Vertical restrictions are disregarded, however, owing to the lack of an internationally accepted theoretical basis. The ICPO would take on the international merger control and the role of abuse commission.

Precisely because of the consequences inherent in such a strategy regarding competition policy, Scherer attempts to save the political feasibility of his plan by incorporating exceptions for sectors[32] of special importance to national interest. Despite this option of exceptions, Scherer's strategy receives the highest rating for allocation efficiency and productive development of competition in relation to the other strategies (+5). The efficiency is accompanied by a considerable interference with national sovereignty (−5), since the national authorities have to take directions from an international authority, and countries not cooperating may have to expect international redress measures on the part of the injured country to be initiated against them. The organizational expense of creating and maintaining an internationally active coordinating and intervening competition authority is very high, especially in comparison with an exclusively decentralized competition policy (−5). A 'super authority' may also be less easily accepted than a decentralized solution because of the recurrent interference in national sovereignty, especially at the beginning (+3). On the other hand, an international and thus objective competition authority would help to even out the unfair economic dominance of the strong countries as perceived by the smaller countries. The WTO mediation procedure is also available, should a country refuse to cooperate on the grounds of national interest. The ICPO has no sanctions instruments of its own. Treating all countries equally is therefore a deciding factor in the acceptance of an international competition authority. The loss of power on the part of the economically dominant countries that would accompany the creation of such an authority can be considered the main hindrance to being able to realize Scherer's strategy politically. An authority that gives directives to national authorities will naturally be vulnerable to more resistance and criticism. It is therefore especially important that the decisions of such an international authority can be so explained as to be understood by all the parties involved. A procedure bound to a set of rules, oriented on an internationally adopted set of competition rules to create transparency and a method of control, is absolutely necessary. Unfortunately, it is unlikely that the international authority would always be able to achieve this ideal constellation.

Although the strategy of Scherer could be characterized as reserved because of the lack of competition policy in international trade, practical thinkers would consider both his scheme and the DIAC to be impossible to realize.[33] From the perspective of competition theory, Scherer is considered wanting. He is also criticized for not addressing price and quota cartels in his strategy as long as they do not represent an import or export cartel, despite the fact that such cartels also restrict market access and worsen both national and international resource allocation. The ICPO could be called upon by a signatory state to act in a case of price and quota cartels, should they restrict market access directly, however.

The option of exempting individual sectors from the anti-trust rule, as well as the absence of a regulation for vertical competition restrictions, are both criticized.[34] The four-digit SITC product categories are too large, which creates substitution relationships between the products that are too weak. In addition, the actual market power with the abuse commission and merger control is not taken into consideration. The regulations of the trade policy sanctions are counterproductive for competition policy, since they create new market access restrictions and thereby make the international resource allocation worse.[35] Alternatives to this strategy would impinge on national sovereignty even more, however. The strategy of Scherer does include merger control and an abuse commission, in contrast to the previously examined strategies, and thus comes closest to the ideal model according to the theory of competition systems. This is why his strategy is awarded in total the highest points for net advantage:

> Whether an option will strengthen the trading system depends importantly on whether: (i) it will reduce the scope for using antitrust to circumvent WTO obligations; and (ii) close other holes and loopholes in existing WTO agreements.[36]

Conclusion

When one regards the strategies for reform of the international system of competition regulation presented in this chapter, it is clear that there is general agreement in the areas of export cartels, mergers and international mediation. Almost all of the strategies suggest an international mediating procedure – as it already exists within the framework of the GATT for trade policy conflicts – for competition policy conflicts as well. Most call for the prohibition of export cartels. An internationally coordinated control is mostly considered necessary for international mergers. For all other competition policy instruments and institutional forms, there seems to be no clear tendency. The comparison between the reform strategies shows that there is a clear trade-off between gained advantage and acceptance on one hand and loss of sovereignty and organizational expense on the other. The international community must decide between the preservation of national individuality (sovereignty) and an undistorted world trade, which means wealth and growth. As everybody knows, it is not possible to have a cake and eat it too. Even though many are not aware of it, the decision was made long ago on the basis of the advanced globalization, which will force an international regulation on competition over the long or short term owing to the unavoidable international conflicts. In November 2001 in Doha, Qatar, the members of the WTO agreed on the start of a new round of trade talks. The intention to begin with talks on international trade regulations is especially important. The behaviour of the politicians follows their own political rationality, however, and not economic rationality.

If one uses the concept of the 'new political economy' to explain the behaviour of politicians, and assumes that politicians want to maximize their own profit above that of the general good, and that being re-elected and the necessary votes to achieve re-election are the top priority, one comes to the conclusion that free trade as a means to an end is clearly inadequate. It can, in fact, have negative consequences. An effective international regulation for competition would remove the many distortions to competition in international trade. This means, though, that the national governments would have to do without many of the instruments with which they now artificially increase the competitiveness of their domestic industry. The individual instruments are mergers, cartels, strategic alliances and vertical relationships, and in general the use of trade restrictions to open markets. Dominant market positions and cartels affect trade directly with discriminatory price-setting, and indirectly by obstructing market access. The national anti-dumping measures, used by states with the intention of smoothing out competition distortions in international trade, can end up having a protectionist effect.[37] Not taking advantage of such a competitive advantage in international trade would probably mean short-term unemployment and thus higher social costs for the state, business closures and perhaps a short-term decrease in the GDP. This would likely lead to a loss of votes and perhaps threaten the re-election chances of the politician since, at the time of the vote, only the costs of fair competition would be seen, and not the profits that would be reaped only over the long-term.[38] The problem is therefore political: it is politically significant whether the competition that squeezes out jobs is domestic or foreign. Politicians tend to favour domestic considerations over foreign in their own interest, despite knowing better than to reject free trade and free market access, as fair and equal competition.[39]

In Doha, the members of the WTO agreed on the start of a new round of trade talks and intended to begin with talks on international trade regulations. However, effective international competition policy actually runs contrary to the interests of many countries. It is therefore anything but given that the WTO states will be able to agree on the targets decided upon in Doha. It is also not a given that they will adopt the necessary competition policies for extensive regulations on competition, which would optimize resource allocation and thus global welfare. The following chapter therefore finally offers strategies as second-best solutions that may not be optimal for competition policy, but are politically feasible and an improvement on the current competition regulations, in case the WTO competition regulations are not realizable. Before this it analyses, on the basis of the concept of the 'new political economy', the interests and motivation of the dominant WTO members as political players representing the interests of their countries.

5

Economic Policy Reform Strategies for International Regulations on Competition

Current interests

There is general agreement between states that the international cooperation of competition authorities and courts should be improved. A general prohibition of hard-core cartels seems to find consensus as well, this being perceptible in the meetings of the WTO working group. At the time of writing, the USA is still contesting the WTO regulations for competition even though the Report of the International Competition Policy Advisory Committee (ICPAC)[1] had already, in April 2000, in large part established the necessity for international rules on competition owing to increasing globalization. The arguments brought by the USA were threadbare at best. One argument was that the WTO has insufficient instruments for intervention and sanctioning, and that US courts could therefore better enforce an international competition policy. Another was that WTO panels lacked the technical expertise necessary to implement an international competition policy. In fact, the USA argued that international competition regulations were unnecessary and their implementation too costly. The USA suspects that their influence on international competition policy could be reduced if there were international rules or if third parties could exert influence. The main fear in this context for the USA is a weakening of its own anti-dumping laws.[2]

Japan and the EU, in contrast, tend to support the extension of WTO competence on competition and would like to go beyond the generally accepted prohibition on hard-core cartels. The EU hopes for restrictions on the extraterritorial application of the US laws based on the effects doctrine, which is in fact applied most often by the USA. The USA even went a step further and utilized the doctrine against Japanese trade branches in the USA in order to keep the Japanese market open for American exports.[3] The EU has for some time entered into bilateral agreements that include trade regulations, such as the free trade agreement with Mexico and South Africa, and thus has built a network of bilateral competition agreements. The EU would prefer to establish rules at the international level in the form of a WTO code within the framework of the Doha world trade round. The basic rules in common would include the non-discrimination principle[4] and transparency. The EU considers transparency especially important, so that market participants can understand the application of laws. The rules of competition should generally match those of the Trips Agreement. Equal rights for domestic and foreign companies to market access are not foreseen, but recourse to national competition courts is to be included. National governments retain control over the implementation of their laws. Using the dispute settlement process has been considered, but only for selected cases as yet unspecified. In addition, the EU wants to see more cooperation between national competition authorities, which would include exchanging information and cooperating on violations that take place across borders, but protecting confidential information would still be allowed. Such cooperation would be on a voluntary basis, and countries would be allowed to exempt branches when signing the agreement, as was proposed by Scherer. Developing countries would receive technical support from industrial countries for the application of the agreement.[5] Like Mexico, the EU strives for an international code that protects against the abuse of market-dominating positions and provides regulation regarding vertical agreements. Mexico considers the standardization of analytical conceptions for national competition authorities and courts to be both desirable and possible.[6]

Canada and Japan, being somewhat less ambitious, have suggested bringing the handling of mergers and market-dominating positions together on an international level. Japan suggests international control of abuse and mergers within the framework of voluntary cooperation between national competition authorities and would like to see anti-dumping proceedings checked, which would clear the way for Japanese exports.[7] Developing countries are supportive of these measures suggested by Canada and Japan, but the EU, as one of the main instigators of anti-dumping procedures, objects to their being checked.[8] Developing countries would generally like to see competition regulated internationally as long as they receive support from industrialized countries. A World Bank report has shown that developing countries are generally the victims in a competition area free of regulation, as can be seen in the example of cross-border cartels.[9]

The USA is meanwhile not exclusively a beneficiary of the competition policy gaps in the GATT; rather, it also has become a victim, which should increase its interest in international rules for competition. The EU has shown, with its successful resistance to the merger of Honeywell and General Electric, that it will enforce its competition policy interests with the effects doctrine just as the USA does, and many transition and developing countries have made it clear with their own initiation of anti-dumping proceedings that the industrial countries will be increasingly affected themselves.

The WTO states cannot therefore be relied upon to come to agreement over the international rules of competition foreseen in Doha.[10] However, because of the different interests it is also questionable as to whether the necessary yet also extensive elements for competition policy presented in this chapter will be agreed upon. The following arguments present a second-best solution in case the desirable competition system cannot become a reality. Such a solution may not be optimal from a competition policy perspective, but it would be politically feasible and would bring about an improvement to the current economic system.

Economic policy reform strategies

Balancing interests

At the time of writing, the economically strong – of course, the USA and the EU – are winning the trade war because of the lack of sanction possibilities. They would also be among the losers were an international competition and trade policy institution capable of asserting itself to be created. This now means that every GATT round or competition regulation either stands or falls according to whether the USA, and also the EU, agrees on it. These two powers dominate the international agenda owing to their economic strength. Whether an agreement or treaty on bilateral trade liberalization has any value depends on the participation of these two parties, because of their huge market potential. The approaches of a League of Nations and of an international competition authority (the ITO) have both failed because of the USA. The US Senate made agreement with the WTO dependent upon the condition that in the first five years after the WTO came into effect, a maximum of two WTO decisions against the USA that did not hold up in US courts would be tolerated, and in this way kept open for itself a door to back out of in the future.[11]

Protectionist companies dominate the lobby scene in the USA and the EU, as in most other countries. The industries oriented towards the domestic economy get their way over the export industries and consumers because they are better organized. The transaction costs theory of the new institutional economy offers an explanation for this phenomenon.[12] The interests of the consumers are opposed to a protectionist policy, since it will increase expenditure and restrict product choice. However, the high transaction and organizational costs of the many consumers prohibit the creation of a lobby interest group. The organizational costs for the producers are conversely much less. There are few producers and many consumers, which is why the profits of protectionism get distributed between few producers and the costs of protectionism distributed across many consumers.[13] In addition, consumers fear that free trade could affect their jobs in the long run, which is why their view dominates the income side. The expenditure side of protectionism is difficult for the individual consumers to determine owing to the number of products that are differently affected. We are also dealing with a public good for consumers when we look at lowered prices through free trade, since those that did not actively work for free trade cannot be excluded from the benefits. The benefit can also be distributed in any manner. For these reasons, the motivation to create a lobby interest group is very low for consumers. That the effect of the many protectionist measures on the overwhelming number of products is very difficult to assess, is another factor.[14]

The reasons for the poor motivation on the part of the consumers also explains the findings of the American International Trade Commission that the total economic costs of the US anti-dumping measures, paid mostly by the consumers, are much greater than the benefits for the protected domestic producers.[15] Free trade is thus a public good which is underestimated by the consumers. The state has to compensate for the 'market failure' of the low interest articulation of the consumers with state-organized consumer groups. In some countries there are consumer associations, but there are as yet no international ones. It is even more difficult for consumers to organize at the international level, owing to the even more confusing number of products and the number of different consumers, whereas producers can build on national organizations already in existence.

Another factor to be considered is that the domestic industries having to compete with imports can pressure politicians by publicly announcing a threatening need to reduce jobs. With the current political power distribution, protectionist interests will tend to dominate negotiations on international competition regulations. Hence, a lobby balance should be created with an international consumer association made up of representatives from national consumer groups; this should be created by parliamentarians where none already exists. The same goes for the export industry. Companies with mostly foreign profits and international companies should compile their interests in an international export association and represent themselves through it.

Interest dividing, or a WTO with two speeds

As already mentioned, a liberal economic system would have little chance of finding the necessary approval from the WTO members, since collective national protectionist interests are currently dominant. This is not the case for all branches, however. Improvement in the sense of a liberal international economic system would be realizable were the current economic system to be separated into its branches, for which there are strong export industry lobbies in the dominating trade blocks of the USA and EU. There is a tendency in these branches for a strong liberalization. There would then be two parts to the WTO with different levels of liberalization, or different 'speeds'.[16]

One can distinguish between different types of branches: depending on the country, there are export-oriented branches for which the foreign exporting industry is the only supplier in the importing country. In such a case, liberalization would not meet resistance from a domestic industry fearing import competition. If the exporting industries are not monopolists in the importing countries, there would be export-oriented industries in other branches of the importing countries that could balance the imports competing with domestic industry with lobby pressure.[17]

This method is that of the liberalization policies of the Uruguay Round and the negotiation strategy of the USA at the beginning of the Millennium Round. With this strategy, however, the liberalization of many sectors is abandoned, and hence the welfare potential of international trade with unfettered access to markets and fair competition is not fully achieved, while resource allocation is left distorted. The consequence is a confusing patchwork of sectors with different levels of liberalization. In the end, such a strategy would signal to countries that exceptions are possible in the concessions to liberalization, and this would not have a positive effect on their willingness to compromise. The EU currently follows a negotiation strategy of both desired and undesired liberalization steps together in package deals for agreement. This strategy has shown the greatest success in the last trade rounds.[18] The protectionist-dominated branches could then be balanced by enough export-oriented branches within the framework of a package-deal vote for the countries to be able to agree to a liberalization. Afterwards, it would be easier to subsume the liberalized branches into an international regulation on competition. Its observance would have to be controlled by the WTO or a similar organization.

An alternative to the strategy of liberalizing sectors or branches at different speeds would be, according to the EU integration strategy, the creation among a small circle of liberal countries of international competition regulations within the framework of the existing WTO. The goal of this strategy would be to unite a critical number of countries, whose economic sphere, taken as an export market, would be so attractive that more and more countries would want to join. This may not be the least of reasons that the sovereignty-conscious United Kingdom joined the EU.

Last but not least, the feasibility of a liberal international competition regulation could be increased if – for example, in Scherer's strategy – every country received the chance to take two existing branches of their choice out of the regulations. Exact criteria would have to be defined for these branches, the observance of which would then naturally be controlled by an international institution.[19]

The property rights strategy for the liberalization of world trade

Many authors, such as Scherer, do not consider it feasible to do away with the currently tolerated international export cartels, owing to the resistance that can be expected from the profiting countries, as long as no compensation is paid. This problem is similar to that at the beginning of the run-up to the early GATT negotiation rounds, with the high import duties then prevalent. It was possible then to convince countries to lower their import duties without direct compensation payments, so the benefits to countries from the GATT negotiations must have outweighed the disadvantages. The same has to be the starting-point for a politically feasible reform strategy of the international competition regulations.

Internationally, governments find themselves in a prisoner's dilemma, since no country liberalizes or gives up protectionist instruments without the security of knowing that others will follow suit; otherwise, they would have to pay the political costs of the structural change induced by foreign trade, without the compensating advantage of free market access for their export industry. This stalemate can be overcome, however, in the sense of the new institutional economy, if a market can be created by the endowment of property rights with appropriate transaction costs (the Coase theorem). The allocation and use of economic goods could be regulated in such a way as to make them beneficial for the general good with property rights.[20]

The economic good that property rights could represent in international trade would be market access by a country. The value of a market access for a particular country depends on the purchasing power of its domestic market and the specific supply-and-demand situation. The value of a market access would depend positively on existing domestic price levels, market volume and exchange rate, and negatively on the demand elasticity and number of domestic suppliers. The value of market access thus varies for each product and is judged differently by the foreign suppliers according to their profit potential. The profit potential for the foreign producers fluctuates with production and transport costs, as well as with the costs of opening up the markets. The transaction costs involved in acquiring product-specific, tradable market access rights should not be higher than the current levying of import duties. Customs officers and ministries would simply have to be assigned to other tasks.

At first glance, this strategy may appear to be just a new face on the old welfare-reducing customs policy, but it is just the opposite in its effect. For a government, the possibility of selling market access represents a source of income that is feasible in the short term, which would give it the necessary incentive to open their markets. The benefit takes a form of income that is recognizable for everyone and is thus a success in terms of political vote maximization.

In contrast to a system of import duties, trade with market access rights does not restrict the free exchange of goods, but rather represents just a partial redistribution of producer profits for the exporters to the importing country. The exporters will only be willing to pay a price that means a profit for them. According to the Coase theorem, resources will be funnelled to the most valuable use independently of the development or distribution of private property rights, but trade must be possible. If exporters have already paid the entire fee, they will use their access privileges all the more intensively, in order to make the costs of market access and the profit margin. The comparative international competitive advantages are already fully used in this area by companies. Since the market access fee is a one-time fee, the surcharge on export prices decreases over time. With adequate competition, the prices will decrease down to the level of the manufacturing and transport costs plus a minimal profit margin. The prices are therefore, in the end, no longer distorted by market access costs, which creates an optimal international resource allocation, so that the comparative cost advantage can be passed on to the consumers.

Preventing states from implementing protectionist instruments after the payment of the market access fee in order to increase the competitiveness of their industries, is decisive for the success of this liberalization strategy. Such prevention can be assured by counting half of the market access fees as payment to the International Monetary Fund. The WTO could then take this investment as a deposit against a case of the proven violation of the rules by a state. Even better would be to limit the market access licences to a reasonable time limit, such as ten years. The possibility of selling the licences anew would then be an incentive to ease market access in the interim, since licence profits could be increased in the future. Ten years is the current time limit for calculation on international capital markets.

The GATT principles as the foundation of an international competition regulation

One could take the position that, in the GATT, the world already has an international competition regulation which only needs to be put into practice. The term 'free trade' implies in principle free, unimpeded trade and thus the absence of any restrictions on contract freedoms or unequal treatment of trading parties. Many restrictions on competition, such as vertical business agreements and cartels, contradict not only the concept of competition policy order in that they restrict market access, but also the principle of free trade. It is thus conceivable that the principles enshrined in the GATT, the 'most favoured nation principle' and the 'national treatment principle' would need to be interpreted in view of competition policy, and implemented with the new WTO mediation mechanism. The WTO Appelate Body stressed the general applicability of Article III of the GATT (the national treatment principle) in 1996. However, it applies only to measures that restrict the import of goods, not to state measures designed to disadvantage foreign companies through competition policy.[21] The 'violation' and the 'non-violation' clauses of Article XXIII (s. 1, a and b) of the GATT could serve as a basis for this process. According to the violation clause, the actions of states can be brought before the mediation board if they hinder the given trade concessions within the framework of the GATT. The non-violation clause states that it is possible to raise a complaint against a GATT member for measures that are not explicitly prohibited, but that impede advantages from trade agreements.[22] The principle of the most favoured nation would mean that competitive concessions provided by a state for its own companies would have to apply for all foreign companies as well. The nation treatment principle would be used as a competition policy principle geared towards equal treatment, under which foreign companies would be placed on an equal footing with domestic companies, including the competition proceedings of national authorities and the access to national competition courts.

Hindley suggests implementing the non-violation clause more stringently, in order to achieve an interpretation from the mediation board that tolerates it; that is to say, that the inaction of the national competition authorities in the case of competition restrictions of foreign countries domestically would be considered measures that violate the GATT.[23] An international competition policy case-law could thus be created.

In the case of *Kodak* v. *Fuji*, the USA used the non-violation clause against the Japanese government with the complaint that they had failed to hinder Fuji from putting pressure on their business partners not to sell Kodak products, in order to prevent Kodak's market entrance. The panel refused the complaint.[24] Until the precedent-setting case of *Kodak* v. *Fuji*, the non-violation clause had never been used to implement competition policy decisions.[25] This may be attributable to the fact that the GATT applies only to signatories, which means states. For the non-violation complaint to have been successful, it would have had to be possible to prove the responsibility of a government for a specific restriction on competition, which includes a predictable disadvantage for a third state. These conditions exist in only a very few cases. The complainant and defendant can also only be governments. Private restrictions on competition are generally left out when it cannot be proven that a government initiated them. The non-violation clause can also only be used in the case of market access restrictions. Other restrictions, such as taking advantage of a dominant market position, remain unaddressed. Last but not least, the panel would not have had the possibility within the framework of the mediation procedure to act directly against the restriction on competition, and could only have empowered the disadvantaged country to take compensation measures, which would not only have left the source of the restriction untouched but would even have worked to increase the distortion in competition.[26]

Despite the identified weaknesses of the clauses in Article XXIII as an instrument of competition policy, the effectiveness of the mediation procedure has been substantially improved in the Uruguay Round. The effectiveness of the clauses was therefore also, at least theoretically, increased, which is why an increased use of the clauses as a complement to other measures is definitely to be recommended.

The minimal consensus

Well-organized international competition would maximize not only global welfare but economic freedom as well. Free access to all markets, the goal of the GATT, would then practically create itself. The current system of world trade desperately needs to be supplemented by a regulated system of competition. Compared with national competition policy standards, an international competition authority would best provide for fair competition and an optimal resource allocation.

Such an authority would come hand in hand with a loss in national sovereignty for states, and would require a relatively harmonized conception of competition. In addition, states would have to give up many instruments of competition policy because they disrupt competition. These instruments are currently used to advance their domestic economies, and national unions can be expected to offer resistance. The probability of politically creating a comprehensive international competition system with an independent competition authority does not seem especially high, and this pessimistic view runs through the academic literature.[27] With the urgent need to reform the international competition system, it would be irresponsible to give up the qualified demands of academics, or to attempt only that which is held to be realistic. Nonetheless, academics should have a common consensus ready as plan B, in order to be able to present a solution should the international negotiations of the next world trade rounds fail to create an international authority.

A common consensus must be able to fulfil the two conflicting goals of optimizing the international system of competition and the political goal of minimal sovereignty loss, at least to the extent that it represents a functional reform strategy. An internationalization of national competition policies is essential in this context. The national competition authorities and courts would be accessible for both foreign countries and companies. Foreign and domestic companies would be treated equally, including dumping measures. According to the model of the GATT, the international community of states must agree at least on ground rules for competition policy that apply for all states, such as the most-preferred-nation principle and the national treatment. The set of rules could be addressed in an annex to the WTO treaties, which is why signing it would be voluntary. States not prepared to give up at least part of their sovereignty for better international market access, or without their own national competition authority, would not be obliged to put the code into force. The incentive to join up would be quite powerful, however, were there a large number of signatory states. In the case of international mergers or competition restrictions, the WTO would have the responsibility to coordinate the inquiries of the national authorities. Clear instructions would be necessary for the national authorities on the commitment to cooperate.

The critical point for this minimal strategy is its implementation by national governments and their authorities, just as it is for the other strategies. Since an international competition authority with its own sanction mechanisms impinges on national sovereignty to a high degree, the reformed mediation instruments from the Uruguay Round offer themselves as an option, to which all parties including private companies should be open. Private parties have no redress measures of their own to implement and are therefore dependent upon their governments. In the production of evidence, they are dependent upon support from domestic and foreign competition authorities. Should insuperable state resistance continue despite this strategy, one could delay the coming into force of such an agreement so far into the future that the politicians who have to decide on the signing of it would no longer have to fear resistance from interest groups and voters in their own term in office.

What will come out of Doha?

At the time of writing it seems as though the WTO will agree on at least a framework agreement on the central hindrances to competition on the basis of international consensus. How the consensual hindrances to competition should be dealt with remains – as in the EU – in the hands of national governments. Horizontal and vertical restrictions on competition are generally considered subjects on which consensus is possible, as long as market prices are directly affected together with general hardcore cartels such as supply and production cartels. It is assumed probable that the WTO competition framework agreement from the dispute settlement process will be excluded, since the WTO states would otherwise fear an attack on their sovereignty. How much application the most-favoured principle would find would then also be a point of contention, since this principle would also include, at least in theory, competition policy concessions in bilateral and regional agreements and thus make them accessible for all WTO members. It is doubtful whether the national-treatment principle would apply in this context, since it would mean equal access for all WTO members to national competition authorities and courts. As has already been shown, access for private individuals – in other words, companies – would be the deciding factor. The competition agreement to emerge from the Doha trade round would therefore fall quite short of the necessities and possibilities of an international competition system as outlined in this book.[28]

There is a clear trade-off between gained advantage and acceptance on the one hand and loss of sovereignty and organizational expense on the other. The international community must decide between sovereignty in connection with advantage – in other words, the preservation of national individuality and world trade – and growth. As everybody knows, it is not possible to have your cake and eat it too. Even though many are unaware of it, the decision was made long ago on the basis of the advanced globalization, which will force an international regulation on competition over the long or short term, owing to the unavoidable international conflicts.

Interviews[1]

Brussels: EU Commission

General Direction I (Foreign Relations)

30.05.1991	18.01.1994	19.04.1994
26.04.1994	02.05.1994	12.07.1995
12.07.1995	13.03.2003*	

General Direction III (Industry)

30.05.1991	18.01.1994	16.03.1994
21.03.1994	28.03.1994	28.03.1994
30.03.1994	30.03.1994	05.04.1994
06.04.1994	07.04.1994	07.04.1994
07.04.1994	11.04.1994	15.04.1994
18.04.1994	25.04.1994	27.04.1994
17.05.1994	18.05.1994	20.05.1994
24.05.1994	25.05.1994	12.07.1995
13.07.1995	13.03.2003*	

General Direction IV (Competition)

19.01.1994	22.03.1994	23.03.1994
28.04.1994	25.05.1994	12.07.1995
13.03.2003*		

General Direction XVI (Regional Policy)

19.05.1994	12.03.2003*

General Direction XII (Science, Research and Development)

19.05.1994

Washington, DC

Public Authorities

US Department of Commerce (International Trade Administration)

31.10.1994	18.11.1994	08.12.1994
08.12.1994	10.03.2003*	

---

* Interviews carried out by telephone.

International Trade Commission

07.11.1994 07.11.1994 15.11.1994
13.03.2003*

US Trade Representative for Industry

22.11.1994 10.03.2003*

EU Trade Delegation

01.11.1994 14.03.2003*

Enterprises

Steel producers

American Iron and Steel Institute
Barry Solarz, vice-president, 10.11.1994
Frank Fenton, senior vice-president, 28.10.1994

NUCOR
Mr Iverson (chairman of the SMA board representative, NUCOR), 01.12.1994*

Steel Manufacturers Association (Minimills)
James Collins (president), 15.11.1994

Steel consumers

Coalition of Steel Using Manufacturers (CASUM)
Bill Lane (manager for international and governmental affairs), 11.11.1994

Coalition of American Businesses for Stable Steel Supplies (CABSSS, Precision Metalforming Association, Pro Trade Group)
Jon Jenson (president), 12.12.1994*

Representative of EU Exporters

International Advisory Services Group
Charles Blum (president), 5.12.1994

American Institute for International Steel
Bess Veig (director), 09.11.1994*

Car traders Nissan and Toyota

22.12.01*

Think tanks and steel experts

The Brookings Institution

Robert Crandall (senior fellow, economic studies programme), 01.11.1994

International trade lawyer

09.11.1994 10.03.2003* 10.03.2003*

Notes

Introduction: On the Way to an International Competition Order

1. See also Petersman (1994), pp. 231–77.
2. See Klodt (2000), p. 53.
3. See Without Author (2000), p. 12.
4. See Bergsten (2000), p. 50; Graham (2000), p. 218; Hindley (2000), pp. 53, 55; Paemen (2000), p. 56; Schott (2000), p. 5.

1 The Theory of Competition Policy: an International Synthesis

1. See Herdzina (1999), p. 9.
2. According to empirical estimations, in a polypoly – as opposed to a monopoly – the static welfare gains in one period alone constitute 10 per cent of the GDP. This is assuming there are no secondary effects. See Scherer (1997), p. 11.
3. This is how the scarcity of a good leads to market position gains, or profit without service. Ordinarily those unable to offer good performance would not be rewarded by the market and would therefore starve. This leads to the question of fairness and the acceptance of a neo-liberal economic system. Fairness is a moral and ethical question, thus at once subjective and not a subject for an economic science text, but rather a philosophical or theological framework. The question of acceptance is decisive for the feasibility of any system, however, and may therefore not be neglected. This was clear in the hefty demonstrations against the expansion of free trade in Seattle 1999.
4. See Berg (1999), p. 233. The Freiburger School sees the equivalent of democracy in individualistically oriented competition, and thus the prevention of a dictator.
5. See Heuβ (1968), p. 29 for the importance of competition for the growth process.
6. See Hayek (1969), p. 249; Starbatty (1987), p. 164.
7. See Schumpeter (1911).
8. For an explanation of *'Schumpeterschen Unternehmers'*, see Dürr (1987), p. 245; Vickers (1994), p. 17.
9. See Drude (1991), p. 7.
10. Empirical proof of the positive effects from import competition on productivity can be found in Baily, Gernsbach, MacDonald and Porter

as well as in the studies from the EU Commission on gains in welfare within the European domestic market. See EU Commission (1988); Porter (1990); MacDonald (1994); Baily and Gernsbach (1995); Scherer (1997).

11. See Conrad (2003a).
12. See Bender *et al.* (1992), pp. 419–48.
13. Vautier (2000), p. 93; OECD (2001), p. 103.
14. The advantages and disadvantages of a global currency would be better analysed in a separate study.
15. Most empirical studies confirm that the dismantling of trade and market access restrictions, and thus an increase in competition, improves the general welfare. The most common term for this is 'globalization'; see McKinnon (2000), p. 11.
16. Scientific and political discussions on the creation of such a competition system have taken place almost exclusively in the USA and Germany; see Kantzenbach and Krüger (1994), p. 196.
17. See Conrad (2003b).
18. See Mantzavinos (1994), p. 160.
19. Eucken's perfect competition does not match the price theory form of perfect competition; see Mantzavinos (1994), p. 76.
20. See Lenel (1989), p. 308.
21. See Starbatty (1983), p. 570.
22. See Starbatty (1983), p. 569; Hildebrand (2002a), p. 160.
23. Eucken does not explicitly use this term himself.
24. See Görgens (1988); Brendel (1997), p. 98.
25. See Starbatty (1983), p. 569; Lenel (1989), p. 309. The seven *constitutive principles* of a competition system are: (1) The creation of a functional price system for perfect competition; (2) Stabilization of the monetary value; (3) Keeping the markets open for new participants; (4) Private property; (5) Contractual freedom; (6) Full responsibility of companies for their decisions; (7) Consistency in competition policy. The four *regulating principles* of competition policy are: (1) The creation of a state monopoly authority; (2) Correction of the economic calculations by integrating external effects; (3) Including anomalies in supply relations, such as on the labour market; (4) Redistribution to achieve social equality. See Eucken (1952).
26. See Hawk (1995), p. 978; Hildebrand (2002a), p. 162.
27. See Lenel (1989), p. 309.
28. See Mason (1939), pp. 61–74.
29. See Clark (1940), pp. 241–56; Aberle (1992), p. 30.
30. See Mason (1939).
31. Different definitions of 'workability competition' can be found in Markham (1950), pp. 348–61; Poeche (1970), pp. 9–32; there is a good summary in Sosnick (1958), pp. 380–423.
32. See Kantzenbach (1967). For a theoretical conception of functional competition, see also Poesche (1970); Mantzavinos (1994), p. 23; Berg (1999), pp. 299–362.

33. This school of thought is represented primarily by Mason and Bain, and by work at Harvard University.
34. In addition, the workability interpretation from Markham should be mentioned, which springs from the idea that optimal competition cannot be achieved, and that competition policy should only intervene until no further improvement in market results can be achieved. Bartling sees the danger in this concept that an uncontrollable, counterproductive intervention will occur. See Bartling (1988), p. 767.
35. See Schüller (1987), p. 58; Bartling (1988), p. 767; Berg (1999); Viscusi *et al.* (2000), p. 62.
36. Structure → behaviour → result; structure → behaviour; behaviour → result; structure → result.
37. On the rule of reason see Schmidt (1981), pp. 282–4.
38. See Hildebrand (2002b), p. 6.
39. See Kowalski (1997); Hildebrand (2002a), p. 130.
40. See Mantzavinos (1994), p. 30.
41. See Mantzavinos (1994), p. 38.
42. See Oberender and Vath (1989), p. 12; Mantzavinos (1994), p. 40.
43. See Hildebrand (2002a), p. 154.
44. See Hayek (1949); Hayek (1969), p. 249; Hayek (1975), p. 15; Hayek (1978), p. 180.
45. See Mantzavinos (2001), p. 212.
46. Even the German Commission of Monopolies was rejected by Hayek because of its discretionary power. See Mantzavinos (1994), pp. 119, 121; Mantzavinos (2001), p. 212; Hildebrand (2002a), p. 154.
47. On the concept of free competition see Hoppmann (1977); Mantzavinos (1994), p. 158.
48. See Schumpeter (1961); Schumpeter (1993), p. 318.
49. According to Hayek, competition is characterized as an experience, to discover facts that would remain hidden without its existence, or at least not used. See Hayek (1969), p. 249; Hayek (1975). For Hayek competition is evolutionary.
50. See Schmidt and Rittaler (1986), p. 767; Schüller (1987), p. 58; Aberle (1992), p. 40.
51. See Posner (1979), pp. 951–2; Shepherd (1990).
52. See Posner (1979), pp. 927, 937. 'The Chicago school does not deny that concentration is a factor that facilitates collusion of a sort difficult to detect, although it attaches less significance to concentration per se than do the oligopoly theories' (op cit., p. 945). Comprehensive literature on intervention criteria in the case of mergers can be found in Stigler (1968), p. 296.
53. Williamson (1968), p. 33; Reder (1982), p. 15; Schmidt and Binder (1996), p. 131. The efficiency-gains are often overevaluated: 60 per cent of American mergers in the early 1990s led to a deterioration of the economic power of the firms. See Sullivan (2002), p. 251.
54. Shepherd (1985), p. 2. See also Hildebrand (2002a), p. 136.

55. See also Glasow (1999), p. 5; Dieckheuer (2002); Hildebrand (2002a), p. 159.
56. This argument can come true only with a price-elastic demand.
57. See Posner (1979), p. 926.
58. The theory of contestable markets should not be put on the same level as the Harvard and Chicago Schools. It is an academic attempt that has never worked in competition practice yet. But the ideas are suitable for the understanding of the different viewpoints on competition of the theory of contestable markets.
59. See Baumol *et al.* (1988); Mantzavinos (1994), p. 56.
60. See Shepherd (1990). '[T]he heroes are the unidentified entrants who exercise discipline over the incumbent, and who do so most effectively when entry is free' (Baumol, 1982, p. 14).
61. See Aberle (1992), p. 40.
62. See Bartling (1997), p. 21.
63. See Pratten (1971); Frohn *et al.* (1973); Grichting (1976); Silberston (1972), pp. 369–91.
64. A comprehensive list of market entrance barriers can be found in Boner and Krueger (1991), p. 6.
65. See Mantzavinos (1994), p. 52.
66. See Mantzavinos (1994), p. 168.
67. 'Thus we must reject as perverse the propensity of regulators to resist the closing down of unprofitable lines of activity. This has gone even so far as a Congressional proposal (apparently supported by Ralph Nader) to require any plant with yearly sales exceeding $250,000 to provide fifty-two weeks of severance pay and to pay three years of taxes, before it will be permitted to close, and that only after giving two years notice!' (Baumol 1982, p. 14).
68. 'In the early 1980s, as part of a plan to free business from excessive government regulation, antitrust was re-engineered from policy that favoured open markets and entrepreneurial opportunity to law narrowly focused on output-limiting conduct that provably raises prices to U.S. consumers' (Fox 1997, p. 10).
69. See Reder (1982), pp. 1–38, esp. 15; Schmidt and Binder (1996), p. 131.
70. See Posner (1979), p. 930.
71. See Nelson (1979), p. 951.
72. Möschel points out that 7 structural market parameters (market share, market entrance barriers, market transparency, cost function, product variation, price elasticity and income elasticity) and 3 values for them (small, middle and large) allows for 116,280 possible combinations. See Möschel (1991), p. 18.
73. See Mantzavinos (1994), p. 137.
74. 'In my view, the ignorance from which we suffer is unavoidable. Economists cannot fill the gap in our knowledge with analytic methods now available to them, and probably will not be able to do so in the future either . . . In fact, the great danger in antitrust today is not that there

will be too little economic analysis, but that there may soon be too much. Just as qualification may create the illusion of certainty, econometric sophistication may provide the illusion of a scientific method' (Ginsburg 1991, p. 28).

75. See Berg (1999).
76. See Kirzner (1992), p. 6; Maks (1995), p. 197; Hildebrand (2002a), p.156.
77. 'The equilibrium is hypothetical, it will never be reached' (Maks 1995, p. 198).
78. See Groeneveld *et al.* (1990), p. 2; Hildebrand (2002a), p. 156.
79. See Kantzenbach (1990), p. 203; Hildebrand (2002a), p. 156.
80. See Mantzavinos (1994), p. 129; Hildebrand (2002a), p. 156.
81. See Maks (1995), p. 198.
82. See Mantzavinos (1994), p. 130; Maks (1995), p. 198.
83. Boner and Krueger (1991, p. 6) offer an extensive listing of market entrance barriers.
84. For instance: EU Commission (1997), para. 24; EU Commission (2001).
85. Hildebrand (2002b), pp. 3–23, esp. 4.
86. The following factors would be analysed by the EC Commission under art. 81(1) EC treaty investigation: (1) Market position of the supplier, of the competitor and of the buyer. (2) Entry barriers. (3) Maturity of the market. (4) Level of trade. (5) Nature of the product and other factors, depending on the case.
87. See Hildebrand (2002b), p. 16.
88. The Chicago School had a large influence on the 'Vertical restraint guidelines' from 1985, which were subsequently removed by the Clinton administration in 1993. See Hildebrand (2002a), p. 152.
89. See Schleicher (1997), p. 310; Hildebrand (2002a), p. 156.
90. See Hovenkamp (1985), p. 256; Hovenkamp (1994); Royal (1995), pp. 445–54, esp. 445; Langlois (2001), p. 200; Hildebrand (2002a), p. 151.
91. See Krattenmaker and Salop (1986), p. 254; Kattan (1993), pp. 1–21; Hovenkamp (1994); Price (1997), pp. 219–54; Schleicher (1997), pp. 311, 315; Langlois (2001), p. 201; Hildebrand (2002a), p. 152.
92. See Hovenkamp (1985), p. 249; Ordover and Willig (1985), p. 311; Schleicher (1997), p. 315; Langlois (2001), p. 202; Hildebrand (2002a), p. 152.
93. See Lande (1989), p. 632; Schleicher (1997), p. 315.
94. See Reder (1982), p. 15; Schmidt and Binder (1996), p. 13.
95. See Möschel (1991), p. 11.
96. Although the concept of the 'economic freedom index' is contested and the results of the studies have varied, the most recent calculations have shown a positive connection between freedom rights and per capita income. See Voigt (2002), pp. 147 f.
97. See *Sachverständigenrat zur Begutachtung der gesamtwirtschaftlichen Entwicklung* (1985), no. 309.
98. See Berg (1988), p. 236.

2 Distortions in Competition: Dumping and Anti-Dumping Measures

1. See Prusa (2001), p. 593.
2. As opposed to 1958 when only 37 anti-dumping proceedings were initiated, the number rose to more than 1456; a breakdown of these shows the USA with 395, the EU 271, Australia 421 and Canada 294. See Horlick (1993), p. 6; Grundlach *et al.* (1995), p. 19.
3. See Ecker (1993), p. 30; Horlick (1993), p. 6; Grundlach *et al.* (1995), p. 19; Prusa (2001), p. 594. For country-specific development of anti-dumping procedures see Leidy (1994).
4. See Hoekman (1997), p. 391; Prusa (2001), p. 592.
5. See Miranda *et al.* (1998), p. 5; Theuringer (2003), p. 6.
6. See Petersmann (1993), p. 62.
7. More than two-thirds of the EU anti-dumping proceedings between 1980 and 1985 were based on the calculated normal value. See Messerlin (1995), p. 43.
8. See Areeda and Turner (1975); Messerlin (1995), p. 42.
9. See for the EC regulation Vander Schueren (1996), p. 279; for the US regulation, Blonigen (2003), p. 5.
10. See Agreement on Implementation of Article VI of the General Agreement on Tariffs and Trade 1994 (henceforth AIA) art. 2, para. 2.2.1, fn. 5.
11. See Kawahito (1982), p. 161; Blonigen (2003), p. 8.
12. Vander Schueren (1996, p. 280) sees this discretionary problem in the new Anti-Dumping Regulation of the EC.
13. See Blonigen (2003), p. 6.
14. AIA VI, art. 2, para. 6.8 as well as appendix II. This interpretation also complies with the decision of the GATT panel in the case of imports of steel containing iron and bismuth from the EU. Conrad (1995).
15. See Knorr (1999), p. 416.
16. See Kulms (1988), p. 207.
17. See Kulms (1988), pp. 78, 204.
18. In the EU Anti-dumping Law, it is laid down that the EU Commission is required to consider general public interests, among them consumer interests, in its final dumping decision. However, in not one of the 903 anti-dumping proceedings in the 1980s was an anti-dumping complaint rejected because of the damaging effects to domestic consumers brought about by the introduction of an anti-dumping duty. See Schuknecht (1992), p. 137.
19. See Vander Schueren (1996), p. 289.
20. See Conrad (1999).
21. See Prusa (2001), p. 602.
22. See Messerlin (1989), p. 586.
23. According to Staiger, Wolak and Messerlin, anti-dumping complaints play a significant role in enforcing price collusions in international cartels.

See Messerlin (1989), pp. 563–87; Staiger *et al.* (1989); Nicolaides (1990), p. 126.
24. See Conrad (1995); Theuringer (2003), p. 60.
25. See Conrad (1995), p. 155.
26. See Prusa (2001), p. 603. Other empirical studies reaffirm that the preliminary anti-dumping duties already have a protectionist effect. See Staiger and Wolak (1994).
27. See Conrad (1995), pp. 155–6.
28. See Petersmann (1993), p. 63; Levonsohn (1994), p. 12; Freytag and Zimmermann (1998), p. 44; Wins (2000), p. 99.
29. See Langer (1995), p. 367.
30. See Conrad (1995).
31. See Kulms (1988), p. 135.
32. See Messerlin and Reed (1995), p. 1567.
33. See Arrow (1969), p. 48.
34. See Frey (1984), p. 25; Glismann *et al.* (1986), p. 138.
35. See Frey (1984), pp. 25, 30.
36. See Conrad (1995).
37. See Conrad (1995).
38. 'Vigorous administration of existing antidumping laws is not procedural protectionism, in my view. Rather, the trade administrators are the real champions of free trade' (Ecker, 1993, p. 34). Alfred Ecker was a commissioner on the US International Trade Commission from 1981 until 1990, and in that time chairman from June 1982 until June 1984.
39. See United States – General Accounting Office (1994), p. 79.
40. See Conrad (1995).
41. The behavioural hypotheses from Smith and Schumpeter took up Downs in the USA and Herder-Dorneich in Germany and thus founded the new political economy. See Downs (1957); Herder-Dorneich (1957); Starbatty (1985), p. 40; Andel (1990), p. 48; Schumpeter (1993), p. 427.
42. See Conrad (1999) and Conrad (2002).
43. See Frey (1984), p. 20.
44. See Herder-Dorneich (1957); Downs (1957).
45. See Zohlnhöfer (1984), pp. 114–15.
46. See United States – General Accounting Office (1994), p. 68.
47. For reciprocal dumping see Brander and Krugman (1983).
48. See Viner (1923); Küng (1975), p. 516; Nicolaides (1990), pp. 116, 123; Van Bael (1990), p. 23.
49. The institutions had to intervene if the selling price was substantially less than the actual market value, and there was the intent of injuring or destroying an industry. See Scherer (1994), p. 83.
50. The OECD analysed 1051 cases of anti-dumping investigations from September 1988 to December 1991. Only in 63 cases was the intent of

destroying and replacing the industry of the importing country even thinkable. See OECD (1996), p. 17.

51. See Ethier (1982), pp. 487–506; Bernhart (1984), pp. 349–70; Hillman and Katz (1986), pp. 403–16; Nicolaides (1990), p. 121.
52. See Conrad (1998).
53. Price policies with the use of contribution margin calculation represent an exception.
54. See Messerlin and Reed (1995), p. 1568.
55. See Feinberg (1989).
56. See Corden (1978); Caves and Jones (1981); Stobbe (1989), p. 200. For the question of sale taxes leading to price differences on the exporting and importing market, which can be regarded as dumping, see Pohmer (1979).
57. See Nicolaides (1990), p. 118.
58. See Nicolaides (1990), pp. 118, 121.
59. See Petersmann (1993), p. 62.
60. See Conrad (1999).
61. See Conrad (1999).
62. See Areeda and Turner (1975); Messerlin (1995), p. 42.
63. See Kulms (1988), p. 207.
64. See Kulms (1988), pp. 78, 204. In the Uruguay Round the lower limit for possible damaging imports was set at a minimum import share of 3 per cent as a threshold. However, in the Dunkel Text, the basis for calculating the negligible share of imports was originally the market and not the import share. This was changed at the insistence of the USA. The odd result is that the more effectively an industry is protected, the larger is the relative import share as a proportion of the total import share and, therefore, determining imports to be non-negligible becomes easier. Furthermore, there is a regulation that allows for an exception: even if the individual import shares of the imports are each less than 3 per cent, an accumulation of imports is permissible if the combined import share of the imports is greater than 7 per cent. This strengthens the tendency towards filing bundled anti-dumping complaints (AIA VI, art. 5, para. 5.8.). See Horlick (1993), p. 14; Horlick and Shea (1995), p. 27; Conrad (1999), p. 124.
65. The EU Anti-dumping Law established that the EU Commission is required to consider general public interests, among which are the consumer interests, in its final decision on dumping. However, in not one of the 903 anti-dumping proceedings in the 1980s was an anti-dumping complaint rejected because of the damaging effects on domestic consumers brought about by the introduction of an anti-dumping duty. See Schuknecht (1992), p. 137.
66. See Nicolaides (1990), pp. 121, 123.
67. See Nicolaides (1990), pp. 118, 121.
68. Sales under variable costs can occur only in exceptional cases, with the exemption of subventions, when surplus is to be cleared.

69. See Petersmann (1993), p. 63.
70. According to Staiger, Wolak and Messerlin, anti-dumping complaints play a significant role in enforcing price collusions in international cartels. See Messerlin (1989), pp. 563–87; Staiger and Wolak (1989); Nicolaides (1990), p. 126.
71. See Conrad (1995).
72. See Conrad (1995), p. 155.
73. See Conrad (1995).
74. See Langer (1995), p. 367.
75. See Conrad (1995).
76. Solvay held 70 per cent of the market share in central Europe in 1990, whereas ICI in the UK has nearly a monopoly.
77. See Motta and Onida (1997), p. 76.
78. See Conrad (1999).
79. See Conrad (2002).
80. See Cass and Boltuck (1996), p. 361; Knorr (1999), p. 417.
81. See Conrad (2002).
82. See Messerlin (2000), p. 159; Prusa (2001), p. 596.
83. Coalition of Steel Using Manufacturers (CASUM) and Coalition of American Businesses for Stable Steel Supplies (CABSSS).
84. See Conrad (1995).
85. See Conrad (1999).
86. See Messerlin (1995), pp. 48, 50.
87. See Hauser and Schoene (1994), p. 214.
88. See Gifford and Matsushita (1996); Gröner and Knorr (1996), p. 586.
89. In the USA, the plaintiff has to prove a significant probability to the court that the defendant accused of dumping is capable of earning the losses caused by the dumping by raising the prices after he has obtained a monopolistic position, which makes it almost impossible (or at least very difficult) for a legal argument on predation to prevail. See Gifford and Matsushita (1996), p. 294; Petersmann (1996), p. 30; Niels and Kate (1997), p. 36.
90. One obstacle will be the fact that a lot of WTO members still lack a domestic competition law. More and more countries are introducing their own competition laws, however, and it would be sufficient if the group of WTO members with their own competition laws and authorities were to start.
91. See Hoekman (1997), p. 400.

3 A Possible Way to an International Competition Order

1. See also Petersmann (1994).
2. See Klodt (2000), p. 53.
3. See Without Author (2000), p. 12.

4. See Boner and Krueger (1991), p. 50; Wins (2000), p. 27. The EU Commission wants new regulations for the cartel prohibition in art. 81 of the EU treaty. In the future, the obligation for cartels to register themselves should be replaced by the legal exception, according to which companies no longer have to report their agreements to the Commission. The cartels would then be valid until the prohibition of the Commission. This would of course make a control of cartels more difficult for the Commission. See Without Author (2002).
5. See Scherer (1997), p. 13.
6. See Gröner (1987), p. 364; Victor (1992), p. 572.
7. See Immenga (1996a), p. 602.
8. See Conrad (2003b).
9. See, for instance, the EU treaty. See Nagy (2002), p. 118; Hildebrand (2002b), p. 18.
10. See World Bank and OECD (1999), p. 29; Morici (2000), p. 29.
11. On the rule of reason see Schmidt (1981).
12. See Wins (2000), p. 149.
13. United Brands versus Commission Case 27/76 (1978) ECR 207 (1978) / CMLR 429. Quoted from OECD (2001), p. 82.
14. See OECD (2001), p. 82.
15. See Fox and Ordover (1995), p. 26; Wins (2000), p. 30; Bridgeman (2002), p. 62. For the abuse control of the EU, see Decker (2000).
16. See FIW (1990), p. 18 f.; Nicolaides (1994a), p. 22; OECD (2001), p. 86.
17. See Holmes (2002), p. 155.
18. Offenders under the Sherman Act can be sentenced to a maximum of three years. See Morici (2000), p. 42.
19. The ECJ recently removed various prohibitions on mergers from the Commission (1990: Airtours–First Choice; 2001: Schneider–Legrand; 2001: Tetra Caval–Sidel), on the ground that mistakes were made in the original calculations of market share. The market share of each of the merged companies was overestimated, and the competition underestimated. In the future, the EU Commission should take possible advantages for consumers from a merger. See Without Author (2001), p. 1 and Morici (2000), p. 31. This is why the USA claims that there is a current trend in European competition policy away from the ordoliberal theory, which aims above all to protect competing companies, towards the model of the USA, which aims to increase consumer welfare through efficiency increases from mergers. See Gifford and Kudrle (2002), p. 233.
20. See Bridgeman (2002), p. 62.
21. See FIW (1990), p. 18; Boner and Krueger (1991), p. 69; Trebilcock (1996), p. 98; UNCTAD (1997), p. 291; Wins (2000), p. 32; Hildebrand (2002b), p. 6 ff.; Bridgeman (2002), p. 60; Nagy (2002), p. 122.
22. See Hay (1993), p. 9; OECD (1996), p. 18; Wins (2000), p. 28.
23. Borrowing from the more fully developed behaviourist workability conception, the EU Commission uses a dynamic market-structure–behaviour–performance theory. Effects that boomerang are taken into consideration, such as the effects of the profitability of a branch (performance) on

market structures over time. The higher the profits, the more likely is the entrance of another company. See Hildebrand (2002b), p. 6.
24. See Conrad (2002).
25. See Gröner (1987), p. 373; OECD (1994a), p. 12; Berg (1999), pp. 309, 350; Herdzina (1999), pp. 46, 52 and 62; Knorr (1999), p. 419; Wins (2000), p. 38.
26. In the USA, the Clayton Act prohibits a monopolistic price differentiation. Such differentiations are allowed only if they correspond to differences in the manufacturing, sales or delivery costs. The market position of the supplier is not of importance in this case. The accused company can exculpate itself if a reasonable price adjustment to the competitors' prices can be proven. In contrast, under the German Act Against Restraints on Competition (ARC) only cartels, market-dominating and price-setting companies are prohibited from price-discrimination (s. 26, para. 2). See Posner (1979), p. 926; Gifford and Matsushita (1996), p. 294; Petersmann (1996), p. 30; Niels and Kate (1997), p. 36.
27. See Duijm and Winter (1994), p. 230; Wins (2000), p. 150.
28. See Conrad (2002).
29. Clayton Act, quoted in Bruns (1969), p. 7.
30. See Conrad (2002).
31. See Niels and Kate (1997), p. 38. Under the condition of a market-dominating position, most anti-dumping duties in the 1980s could not have been imposed. See Knorr (1999), p. 426.
32. See Immenga (1996a), p. 605.
33. See Goldfarb (1995), p. 126; Herdzina (1999), p. 157.
34. See Matshushita (1995), p. 129; Sadao and Goto (1997), p. 23.
35. See Tirole (1998), ch. 4.
36. See Kühn *et al.* (1992), p. 14; Motta and Onida (1997), p. 604.
37. This is, above all, the view of the Chicago School. See Posner (1979), p. 927.
38. See Viscusi *et al.* (2000), p. 236.
39. See also Boner and Krueger (1991), p. 57; Kühn *et al.* (1992), p. 14.
40. See Viscusi *et al.* (2000), p. 236.
41. See Boner and Krueger (1991), p. 57; Carlton (1994), pp. 544, 845; Nicolaides (1994), p. 21; Fox and Ordover (1995), p. 24; Wins (2000), p. 29. For a complete analysis of the EU competition policy on vertical relationships, see Duijm (1997).
42. See Immenga (1996a), p. 604.
43. The EU Commission has also chosen to consider possible competition hindrances with the rule of reason, which might include advantages resulting from vertical agreements in the form of efficiency gains. They consider the following aspects under art. 81(1) of the EC treaty: (1) The market position of the supplier, competitors and consumers; (2) Market entry barriers; (3) The maturity of the market; (4) The extent of trade; (5) The type of product. There are also other factors depending on the case. See Petersmann (1996), p. 10; Hoekman (1997), p. 396; Brinker (1999), pp. 62, 64; Hildebrand (2002b), p. 16. The EU Commission stresses that a vertical restriction can come about only if there is a lack of inter-brand competition

or the agreements have a market share of more than 20 per cent. See Brinker (1999), p. 64; Morici (2000), p. 31. See Duijm (1997) and Hildebrand (2002b), p. 16 for the way the EC Commission has dealt with vertical restrictions on competition.

44. See World Bank and OECD (1999), p. 44.
45. See Hagedoorn (1996); Klodt (2000), p. 53.
46. According to the so-called effects doctrine, the national competition law can be used against all restrictions on competition by both domestic and foreign companies if they have an impact on the domestic market. Here, we are dealing with a legal basis used especially by the USA and internationally is hotly disputed. See Rishikesh (1991), p. 34; Immenga (1996a), p. 596; Immenga (1996b), p. 156; Pengilley (1997), p. 22.
47. The effects doctrine was used in the USA for the first time in 1945. In the so-called Alcoa Case under the Sherman Antitrust Act, the US Supreme Court forbade a quota cartel of foreign aluminium producers that had determined the quotas for the US market in Switzerland. See Klodt (2003), p. 46. Klodt puts together the most important application of the effects doctrine. The overview can be found in Table 4.3.
48. See Motta and Onida (1997), p. 83.
49. See Without Author (2000), p. 12.
50. See Van Miert (1996), p. 3.
51. See Wins (2000), p. 31.
52. See Wins (2000), p. 31.
53. See FIW (1990), p. 18; Trebilcock (1996), p. 98; Wins (2000), p. 32. Boner provides a description of the national merger control mechanisms. See Boner and Krueger (1991), p. 69.
54. See Schüller (1987), p. 58.
55. See Wins (2000), p. 32.
56. See Neven and Siotis (1993), p. 89.
57. See Motta and Onida (1997), p. 89.
58. See also Kühn *et al.* (1992), p. 28.
59. See especially Campbell and Trebilcock (1997) for more on the difficulties of a border-crossing merger.
60. See Subramanian (1994); Boner and Krueger (1991). Also, the EU comes to this conclusion: 'However, it should be noted that the diversity of national competition laws – while important – is not to be exaggerated. There is a core of commonality regarding a number of the key elements of competition law and policy. If one analyses the nearly 100 existing competition law regimes, a high degree of convergence can be detected regarding the following main characteristics of competition law and policy despite differences on substantive provisions and institutional structures . . .'. See Working Group on the Interaction between Trade and Competition Policy (2002b), p. 1.
61. See also Hauser and Schoene (1994); Noland (1999); Plompen (2001), pp. 31 f.
62. See Immenga (1996a), p. 602.

63. 'But such reforms, even though they would enhance national welfare and due process of law, are unlikely to come about through unilateral reforms or through negotiations between the representatives of the antidumping bureaucracies' (Petersmann, 1993, p. 63).
64. See Hauser and Schoene (1994).
65. See Freytag and Zimmermann (1998), p. 49.
66. A constant stream of states join the WTO. The GATT had 85 signatories in 1980, and, in 1999, 134 states had joined the WTO. See World Bank (2000), p. 7. In 2004, the WTO had 147 members.
67. Scherer provides many examples. See Scherer (1997), p. 5.
68. The EU commission refrained from an extraterritorial application of their law in the case of the foreseen merger between Boeing and McDonnell Douglas (under the pretence of a concession), despite the negative comity of nations, not least of all due to the threat of trade policy sanctions from the USA. The merger between General Electric and Honeywell was prevented by the EU, however, despite bitter resistance from the USA. See Wins (2000), pp. 82, 88; Without Author (2001), p. 13.
69. See Hauser and Schoene (1994), p. 219.
70. Neven and Siotis (1993, pp. 87, 89) say mainly the same.
71. See Schüller (1987), p. 61.

4 Strategies to Reform the Regulations on International Competition

1. See Giardina and Zampetti (1997), pp. 5–27.
2. See Mattoo and Subramanian (1997), pp. 96–115.
3. See Hauser and Schoene (1994), pp. 205–22.
4. See Hauser and Schoene (1994); Hoekman and Mavroides (1994).
5. See Conrad (2002), pp. 563–75.
6. See Gröner (1987), p. 365; Duijm and Winter (1993), p. 466; Vermulst (1993), p. 7; WTO (1997), pp. 31, 55; Monopolkommission (1998), p. 27; Wins (2000).
7. See Blackhurst (1994), pp. 223–9; Immenga (1995), pp. 1–16. The EU Commission demands defensive measures against strategic alliances of foreign companies and at the same time supports the creation of strategic alliances between European firms. See Grundlach *et al.* (1995), p. 26.
8. See Conrad (1999), pp. 123–33.
9. See Klodt (2003), pp. 57, 66.
10. See Hauser and Schoene (1994), p. 212.
11. The new Subsidies Code from the Uruguay Round of the GATT incorporates several improvements. Various forms of subsidies have been classified for the first time, and respective allowable retaliation measures have been defined. The breakthrough was made possible by the organization of the different forms of subventions into three categories: (1) 'red light category' or forbidden or export subsidies; (2) 'yellow light category'

or actionable subsidies; (3) 'green light category' or non-actionable subsidies (meanwhile the green light category expired).

12. See Mattoo and Subramanian (1997).
13. See Subramanian (1994).
14. See OECD (1994b).
15. 'International comity' is generally understood to be the politeness of states in their dealings with one another, as well as the information of foreign countries of extraterritorial application of rules. The French term *'courtoisie'* is also commonly used. See Vermulst (1993), p. 11; Jakob-Siebert (1996), p. 63; Wins (2000), p. 79.
16. That negative comity is not obligatory is clear when national interests are at stake. Thus, the EU Commission did not want to give up an extraterritorial application of its laws in the case of the merger between Boeing and McDonnell, even though the US competition authorities (Federal Trade Commission) had already approved the merger. See Van Miert (1996), p. 3; and Wins (2000).
17. See Immenga (1996a), p. 162; Jakob-Siebert (1996), p. 63; Hoekman (1997), p. 385; Wins (2000), p. 87.
18. See Gröner (1987), p. 369; Rishikesh (1991), p. 60; Atwood (1993), p. 87; EU Commission (1995), p. 13; Immenga (1996b), pp. 157, 163; Van Miert (1996), p. 3; Starek (1996), p. 36; Trebilcock (1996), p. 90; Wins (2000), p. 85.
19. Many participants of the bilateral competition agreement fear that the USA could use it to increase its extraterritorial influence. In one case, the USA even acted unilaterally against Australian and Canadian companies, which is why both latter governments make use of the blocking status by directing their enterprises to refuse cooperation with the US authorities (blocking status). See Hermanns (1989), p. 448; EU Commission (1995), p. 15; Wins (2000).
20. Schmidt (1981), pp. 282–4.
21. Eleanor M. Fox is Walter J. Derenberg Professor of Trade Regulation at New York University.
22. Janusz A. Ordover is Professor of Economics at New York University. Affiliations: American Economic Association; American Bar Association; Former Deputy District Attorney General, US Department of Justice; Special Adviser to the Organization for Economic Cooperation and Development (OECD) and the World Bank.
23. See Fox and Ordover (1995), p. 16.
24. See Fox and Ordover (1995); Wins (2000), p. 132.
25. U. Immenga, F. Jenny and E. U. Petersmann.
26. See EU Commission (1995).
27. The non-compulsory competition policy suggestions of the OSCE and UNCTAD had no effect, for example. See Fox (1997), p. 2; Wins (2000), p. 131.

28 See Fikentscher and Immenga (ed.) (1995).

29. See Gröner and Knorr (1996).
30. See Phillips (1994), pp. 327–48; Fikentscher and Drexl (1995), pp. 35–52; Klodt (1995), pp. 15–26; Fikentscher (1996), p. 156; Krüger (1996), pp. 219–29; Mattoo and Subramanian (1997), p. 96; Wins (2000), p. 122.

31. Scherer works as a consultant to states on questions of national and international competition and teaches at Harvard University. He supports the competition policy concept of the Harvard School (Scherer 1994). For more details, see Hoekman (1997), pp. 383–406.
32. As examples Scherer gives Brazil's international coffee cartel, OPEC, Canada's export cartel for potash and uranium, Russia's cooperation with the De Beer diamond syndicate and Boeing's dominance in large passenger planes. The last example as an export cartel (more of a monopoly really) could soon ended by the extended product supply from Airbus.
33. When Scherer presented his paper at a conference in Washington, DC in 1995, a judge countered him that the world would accept Esperanto as a common language before they would accept his suggestion for an international system of competition. See Scherer (1997).
34. See Hoekman (1997), p. 385; Wins (2000), p. 126.
35. See Duijm and Winter (1992), p. 374; Hoekman (1997), p. 385; Wins (2000), p. 126.
36. Hoekman (1997), p. 397.
37. See Conrad (1999); Conrad (2002).
38. See Frey (1984), p. 20.
39. See Zohlnhöfer (1984), pp. 114–15.

5 Economic Policy Reform Strategies for International Regulations on Competition

1. The ICPAC was given the task of analysing the international competition system by the American government. Despite the weaknesses that were determined, a system for competition within the framework of the WTO was rejected. See Holmes (2002), p. 169.
2. See Bergsten (2000), p. 50; Graham (2000), p. 218; Hindley (2000), pp. 53, 55; Paemen (2000), p. 56; Schott (2000), p. 5.
3. See Scherer (1997), p. 14; Nicolaides (2001), p. 139.
4. National-treatment principle and most-favoured-nation principle.
5. See Scherer (1994); Pons (1999); Plompen (2001), p. 32; Hindley (2002), p. 157; Holmes (2002), p. 167; Working Group on the Interaction between Trade and Competition Policy (2002b); Conrad (2003b).
6. See Bergsten (2000), p. 50; Graham (2000), p. 218; Hindley (2000), pp. 53, 55; Paemen (2000), p. 56; Schott (2000), p. 5; Nicolaides (2001), p. 139; Holmes (2002), pp. 155, 169; Vautier (2002), p. 10.
7. See OECD (2000), p. 79; Working Group on the Interaction between Trade and Competition Policy (2002a).
8. See Bergsten (2000), p. 50; Graham (2000), p. 218; Hindley (2000), pp. 53, 55; Paemen (2000), p. 56; Schott (2000), p. 5; Nicolaides (2001), p. 139; Holmes (2002), p. 155, 169; Vautier (2002), p. 10.
9. See Petersmann (1999), p. 60; Holmes (2002), p. 159.
10. Several of the experts in Washington and Brussels currently interviewed said that in their estimation no competition rules of any kind will be agreed upon.

11. See Dell (1990), p. 8; Scherer (1994), p. 38; Graham (1996), p. 110; Scherer (1994), p. 13; See Scherer (1997), pp. 14, 18; Beise (2001), p. 36. Surprisingly enough, the interpretation in the German literature is that the USA failed to ratify the Havana Charter because the liberalization was not far-reaching enough for them. See Wolany (1958), p. 528; Mozet (1991), p. 17. The truth is that not ratifying the Havana Charter prevents an international system of competition and leaves the USA a legal vacuum in which to act.
12. See Arrow (1969), p. 48.
13. See Frey (1984), p. 25; Glismann *et al.* (1986), p. 138.
14. See Frey (1984), p. 25.
15. See Bronckers (1996), p. 18.
16. The agreements for the telecommunications sector within the GATT contain rules for competition, for example.
17. See a similar proposal from Petersmann (1993), p. 63. Petersmann is optimistic about the feasibility of such a proposal to combine the GATT's practical experience with liberalizing and harmonization: 'national foreign trade laws suggests that an international harmonization of competition laws will succeed, if at all, only on the basis of overall reciprocity and as part of a more comprehensive international package deal'. See Petersmann (1993), p. 65.
18. See Koopmann *et al.* (1999), p. 648.
19. Hoekman (1997, p. 402) also credits sector-specific liberalization with a generally greater chance of being realized.
20. See Coase (1969); Furubotn and Pejovich (1972), p. 1139; Richter and Furubotn (1999), p. 82; Martiensen (2000), p. 252; Voigt (2002), p. 68. For the use of the Coase theorem with public goods, see Demsetz (1970); Oakland (1974); Endres (1980); Endres (1981).
21. See Holmes (2002), p. 159.
22. See also Hoekmann and Mavroidis (1994), p. 19; Mavroidis and Van Siclen (1997), p. 10.
23. See Hindley (1996), p. 339.
24. One reason may have been that Agfa succeeded in establishing itself in the market due to a good business strategy, in contrast to Kodak. See Wins (2000), p. 102. WTO panel, Report of the WTO panel, Japan – Measures Affecting Consumer Photographic Film and Paper, WT/DS44/R, para. 10.388 (adopted April 22, 1998).
25. See Hoekman (1997), p. 386.
26. See Hauser and Schoene (1994), p. 208; Hoekman (1994), p. 10; Nicolaides (1994b), p. 214; Hawk (1996), p. 10; Vermulst (1999), p. 15; Wins (2000), P. 101.
27. *'Es erscheint nicht nur gegenwärtig, sondern auch auf absehbare Zeit ausgeschlossen, den globalen Wettbewerb einer Rechtsordnung zu unterstellen.'* ('It seems not only at the moment out of the question to subject global competition to a legal system, but not even in the near future.') (Immenga 1996a, p. 599).

28. See Kennedy (2001) and Holmes (2002), p. 158. Plompen considers access for private parties to national competition courts to be possible. It is critical, however, that there be a general freedom from obligation. See Plompen (2001), p. 33.

Interviews

1. Unfortunately most interviewees wished to remain anonymous.

References

Aberle, Gerd (1992) *Wettbewerbstheorie und Wettbewerbspolitik*, Stuttgart.

Andel, Norbert (1990) *Finanzwissenschaft*, 3rd edn, Tübingen.

Areeda, R. and Turner, D. (1975) 'Predatory Pricing and Related Practices Under Section 2 of the Sherman Act', *Harvard Law Review*, vol. 88, no. 4, pp. 697–733.

Arrow, K. J. (1969) 'The Organization of Economic Activity: Issues Pertinent to the Choice of Market versus Non-Market Allocation', in: *The Analysis and Evaluation of Public Expenditures: The PBB-System*, Joint Economic Committee, 91st Congress, 1st Session, vol. 1, Washington, DC, pp. 47–64.

Atwood, James R. (1993) 'Positive Comity – Is It a Positive Step?', in: Hawk, Barry E. (ed.), *International Antitrust Law and Policy*, New York, pp. 79–89.

Bael, Ivo v. and Bellis, Jean-François (1985) *EEC and Other Trade Protection Laws*, London.

Baily, Martin and Gernsbach, Hans (1995) 'Efficiency in Manufacturing and the Nature of Competition', in: *Brookings Papers on Economic Activity*, Microeconomics, pp. 307–58.

Bartling, H. (1988) 'Wettbewerbstheorie', in: Woll, Artur (ed.), *Wirtschaftslexikon*, 3rd edn, Munich, pp. 768–77.

Bartling, Hartwig (1997) 'Von der Wettbewerbstheorie zur Theorie der Wettbewerbspolitik', in: Kruse, Joern (ed.), *Wettbewerbspolitik im Spannungsfeld nationaler und internationaler Kartellrechtsordnungen, Festschrift für Ingo Schmidt zum 65,* Geburtstag, Baden-Baden, pp. 17–31.

Baumol, William J. (1982) 'Contestable Markets: An Uprising in the Theory of Industry Structure', *American Economic Review*, vol. 72, no. 1, pp. 1–5.

Baumol, William J., Panzar, John C. and Willig, Robert D. (1988) *Contestable Markets and the Theory of Industry*, San Diego.

Beise, Marc (2001) *Die Welthandelsorganisation* (WTO), Baden-Baden.

Bender, Dieter, Berg, Hartmut, Cassel, Dieter, Claassen, Emil-Maria (1992) 'Außenhandel', in: Bender, Dieter a.o. (ed.), *Vahlens Kompendium der Wirtschaftstheorie und Wirtschaftspolitik*, 5th edn, Munich, pp. 419–77.

Berg, Hartmut (1988) 'Wettbewerbspolitik', in: Bender, Dieter, Berg, Hartmut, Cassel, Dieter and Claassen, Emil-Maria (eds), *Vahlens Kompendium der Wirtschaftstheorie und Wirtschaftspolitik*, pp. 230–91.

Berg, Hartmut (1999) 'Wettbewerbspolitik', in: Bender, Dieter a.o. (ed.), *Vahlens Kompendium der Wirtschaftstheorie und Wirtschaftspolitik*, vol. 2, 7th edn, Munich, pp. 299–362.

Bergsten, C. Fred (2000) 'The United States' Interest in New Global Trade Negotiations', in: Schott, Jeffrey J. (ed.), *The WTO after Seattle*, Washington DC, pp. 43–52.

Bernhardt, Dan (1984) 'Dumping, Adjustment Costs and Uncertainty', *Journal of Economic Dynamics and Control*, vol. 8, no. 3, pp. 349–70.

Blackhurst, R. (1994) 'Competition Policies: National Versus Multinational Jurisdiction', *Aussenwirtschaft*, vol. 49, no. 2, pp. 223–9.

Blonigen, Bruce A. (2003) *Evolving Discretionary Practices of U.S. Antidumping Activity*, National Bureau of Economic Research, Working Paper No. 9625, Cambridge, MA, April.

Bohnert, Walter and Reising, Susanne (1990) *Zur aktuellen Lage auf dem Weltstahlmarkt. Strukturelle Krise und diskretionäres Mismanagement*, Arbeitspapier FU Berlin – Fachbereich Politische Wissenschaft, no. 1, pp. 38.

Boner, Alan Roger and Krueger, Reinald (1991) *The Basis of Antitrust Policy: A Review of Ten Nations and the European Communities*, World Bank Technical Paper no. 160, Washington, DC.

Brander, James and Krugman, Paul (1983) 'A Reciprocal Dumping Model of International Trade', *Journal of International Economics*, vol. 15, no. 314, pp. 313–21.

Brendel, Herwig (1997) 'Wettbewerbspolitische Konzeptionen, Positive Theorie in normativer Einbindung', in: Delhaes, K. von and Fehl, U. (ed.), *Dimensionen des Wettbewerbs, Schriften zu Ordnungsfragen der Wirtschaft*, vol. 52, Stuttgart, pp. 79–101.

Bridgeman, John (2002) 'International Mergers and Acquisitions', *European Business Journal*, vol. 14, no. 2, pp. 58–62.

Brinker, Ingo (1999) 'Vertikale Wettbewerbsbeschränkungen – Anmerkungen zum neuen Regelungsansatz der Kommission', in: Schwarze, Jürgen (ed.), *Neuere Entwicklungen auf dem Gebiet des europäischen Wettbewerbsrechts*, Baden-Baden, pp. 59–70.

Bronckers, Marco C. E. (1996) 'Rehabitating Antidumping and other Trade Remedies through Cost-Benefit Analyses', *Journal of World Trade*, vol. 30, no. 2, pp. 5–35.

Bruns, Joseph W. (1969) *Antitrust Dilemma: Why Congress Should Modernize the Antitrust Laws*, New York.

Campell, A. Neil and Trebilcock, Michael J. (1997) 'Interjurisdictional Conflicts in Merger Review', in: Waverman, Leonard, Comanor, William, S. and Goto, A. (eds), *Competition Policy in the Global Economy: Modalities for Cooperation*, London, pp. 89–126.

Carlton, Dennis W. (1994) *Modern Industrial Organization*, New York.

Cass, Ronald A. and Boltuck, Richard D. (1996) 'Antidumping and Countervailing-Duty Law: The Mirage of Equitable International Competition', in: Bhagwati, Jagdish and Hudec, Robert E. (eds), *Fair Trade and Harmonization: Prerequisites for Free Trade?*, Massachusetts Institute of Technology, Boston, MA, pp. 351–414.

Caves, R. E. and Jones, R. W. (1981) *World Trade and Payments – An Introduction*, Boston, MA.

Clark, J. M. (1940) 'Towards a Concept of Workable Competition', *American Economic Review*, vol. 30, no. 2, pp. 241–56.

Conrad, Christian A. (1995) 'Steel: A New Round of Protectionism in American Trade', *Intereconomics*, vol. 30, no. 3, pp. 150–6.

Conrad, Christian A. (1998) 'Antidumping nach der Uruguay-Runde', *List Forum*, vol. 24, no. 3, pp. 261–78.

Conrad, Christian A. (1999) 'Balancing the GATT Antidumping Code', *World Competition*, vol. 22, no. 2, pp. 123–33.

Conrad, Christian A. (2002) 'Dumping and Anti-Dumping Measures from a Competition and Allocation Perspective', *Journal of World Trade*, vol. 36, no. 3, pp. 563–75.

Conrad, Christian A. (2003a) 'Außenwirtschaftliche Marktmechanismen zur Integration der Weltwirtschaft', *WiSt* (*Wirtschaftswissenschaftliches Studium*), vol. 32, no. 6, pp. 345–50.

Conrad, Christian A. (2003b) 'Strategies to Reform the Regulations on International Competition', *World Competition*, vol. 26, no. 1, pp. 101–21.

Corden, W. M. (1978) *Trade Policy and Economic Welfare*, Oxford.

Decker, Eric (2000) *Das Europäische Mißbrauchsverbot im Verhältnis zu den Immaterialgüterrechten*, Dresden.

Dell, Sidney (1990) *The United Nations and International Business*, London.

Demsetz, H. (1970) 'The Private Production of Public Goods', *The Journal of Law and Economics*, vol. XIII, no. 2, pp. 293–306.

Deutscher Bundestag (Enquete-Kommission 'Globalisierung der Weltwirtschaft – Herausforderungen und Antworten') (2002) *Abschlussbericht*, 24 June.

Dieckheuer, Gustav (2002) 'Competition, Environment and Trade in the Globalized Economy', in: Koehler, Thomas and Kooths, Stefan (eds), *Preparing a World Antitrust Framework: An Ordoliberal Approach*, Frankfurt, pp. 49–65.

Downs, Anthony (1957) *An Economic Theory of Democracy*, New York.

Drude, Michael (1991) 'Walter Eucken – Ein Wegbereiter des "Deutschen Wunders"', in: *Industrie- und Handelskammer Nordschwarzwald (Pforzheim): Informationen für die Wirtschaft*, no. 4, pp. 56–77.

Duijm, Bernhard (1997) *Die Wettbewerbspolitik der EG gegenüber vertikalen Vertriebsvereinbarungen*, Baden-Baden.

Duijm, Bernhard and Winter, Helen (1992) 'Für eine neue Dimension der Handelspolitik', in: *Wirtschaftsdienst*, vol. 72, no. VII, pp. 374–9.

Duijm, Bernhard and Winter, Helen (1993) 'Internationale Wettbewerbsordnung – Alternativen und ihre Probleme', *Wirtschaft und Wettbewerb*, vol. 43, no. 6, pp. 465–74.

Duijm, Bernhard and Winter, Helen (1994) 'Möglichkeiten und Grenzen einer internationalen Wettbewerbsordnung', in: Vitzthum, Wolfgang Graf (ed.), *Europäische und Internationale Wirtschaftsordnung aus der Sicht der Bundesrepublik Deutschland*, Baden-Baden, pp. 225–47.

Dürr, Ernst (1987) 'Der Schumpeterische Unternehmer in der Theorie der wirtschaftlichen Entwicklung', in: Borchert, Manfred, Fehl, Ulrich and Oberender, Peter (eds), *Markt und Wettbewerb – Festschrift für Ernst Heuß zum 65. Geburtstag*, Bern, pp. 245–63.

Ecker, Alfred, E. (1993) 'Antidumping after the Uruguay Round: A Former Administrator's Perspective', in: Kreinin, Mordechai E. (ed.), *International Commercial Policy*, Washington, DC, pp. 29–35.

Endres, A. (1980) 'Second Hand Markets and the Private Supply of Excludable Public Goods', *Public Finance*, vol. 36, no. 2, pp. 227–38.

Endres, Alfred (1981) 'Neuere Entwicklungen in der Theorie der öffentlichen Güter', in: *Zeit chrift für die gesamte Staatswissenschaft*, vol. 137, no. 1, pp. 134–49.

Ethier, W. (1982) 'Dumping', *Journal of Political Economy*, vol. 90, no. 3, pp. 487–506.

Eucken, Walter (1952) *Grundsätze der Wirtschaftspolitik*, Tübingen.

EU Commission (1988) *Research on the 'Costs of Non-Europe': Basic Findings*, Luxembourg: Publications Office of the European Communities.

EU Commission (ed.) (1995) *Competition Policy in the New Trade Order: Strengthening International Cooperation and Rules*, Brussels/Luxembourg.

EU Commission (1997) *Notice on the Definition of the Relevant Markets*, OJ C 372/5, 9 December 1997, paragraph 24.

EU Commission (2001) *Green Paper on the Review of Council Regulation (EEC)*, No. 4064/89, Com (2001) 745/6 final, Brussels, 11 December 2001.

EU Commision (2002) *Responses to the Challenges of Globalisation: A Study on the International Monetary and Financial System and Financing for Development*, Brussels, 13 Feburary 2002, SEC (2002) 185 final.

Feinberg, Robert M. (1989) 'Exchange Rates and "Unfair Trade"', *Review of Economics and Statistics*, vol. 71, no. 4, pp. 704–7.

Fikentscher, Wolfgang (1996) 'Multilaterale Regeln für den internationalen Wettbewerb?', in: Kantzenbach, Erhard and Mayer, Otto G. (eds), *Von der internationalen Handels- zur Wettbewerbsordnung*, Baden-Baden, pp. 159–218.

Fikentscher, Wolfgang and Drexl, Josef (1995) 'Der Draft International Antitrust Code – Zur institutionellen Struktur eines künftigen Weltkartellrechts', in: Fikentscher, Wolfgang and Immenga, Ulrich (eds), *Draft International Antitrust Code*, Baden-Baden, pp. 35–52.

Fikentscher, Wolfgang and Heinemann, Andreas (1994) '"Der Draft International Antitrust Code" – Initiative für ein Weltkartellrecht im Rahmen des GATT', *Wirtschaft und Wettbewerb*, vol. 44, no. 2, pp. 97–107.

Fikentscher, Wolfgang and Immenga, Ulrich (eds) (1995) *Draft International Antitrust Code*, Baden-Baden.

FIW (ed.) (1990) *Internationale Zusammenschlüsse und Wettbewerbspolitik*, FIW-Dokumentation H. 13, Cologne.

Fox, Eleanor M. (1986) 'Monopolization and Dominance in the United States and the European Community: Eficiency, Opportunity, and Fairness', *Notre Dame Law Review*, vol. 61, no. 5, pp. 981–1020.

Fox, Eleanor M. (1997) 'Toward World Antitrust and Market Access', *American Journal of International Law*, vol. 91, no. 1, pp. 1–25.

Fox, Eleanor, M. and Ordover, Janusz A. (1995) 'The Harmonization of Competition and Trade Law. The Case for Modest Linkages of Law and Limits to Parochial State Action', *World Competition*, vol. 19, no. 2, pp. 5–34.

Frey, Bruno S. (1984) 'Die Politische Ökonomie des Protektionismus', *Aussenwirtschaft*, vol. 39, no. 1/2, pp. 17–42.

Freytag, Andreas and Zimmermann, Ralf (1998) 'Muß die internationale Handelsordnung um eine Wettbewerbsordnung erweitert werden?', *Rabels Zeitschrift für ausländisches und internationales Privatrecht*, vol. 62, no. 1, pp. 38–58.

Frohn, J., Krengel, R., Kuhbier, P., Oppenländer, K. H. and Uhlmann, L. (1973) *Der technische Fortschritt in der Industrie*, Berlin.

Furubotn, E. G. and Pejovich, S. (1972) 'Property Rights and Economic Theory: A Survey of Recent Literature', *Journal of Economic Literature*, vol. 10, no. 4, pp. 1137–62.

Giardina, Andrea and Zampetti, Beviglia (1997) 'Settling Competition-Related Disputes – The Arbitration Alternative in the WTO Framework', *Journal of World Trade*, vol. 31, no. 6, pp. 5–27.

Gifford, Daniel J. and Kudrle, Robert T. (2002) 'Alternative National Merger Standards and the Prospects for International Cooperation', in: Kenneda, Daniel L. M. and Southwick, James D. (eds), *The Political Economy of International Trade Law: Essays in Honour of Robert E. Hudec*, Cambridge, pp. 208–47.

Gifford, Daniel J. and Matsushita, Mitsuo (1996) 'Antitrust or Competition Laws Viewed in a Trading Context: Harmony or Dissonance?', in: Bhagwati, Jagdish and Hudec, Robert E. (eds), *Fair trade and Harmonization: Prerequisites for Free Trade?*, Massachusetts Institute of Technology, Cambridge, MA, pp. 269–331.

Ginsburg, Douglas H. (1991) 'Comment: The Goals of Antitrust Revisited', *Journal of Institutional and Theoretical Economics*, vol. 147, no. 1, pp. 24–30.

Glasow, Bernhard (1999) *Vertikale Preisbindung, Wettbewerbstheorie und Wettbewerbsrecht in den USA, Deutschland und Europa*, Frankfurt.

Glismann, Hans Hinrich, Horn, Ernst-Jürgen and Sighard Nehring (1986) *Weltwirtschaftslehre I: Außenhandels- und Währungspolitik*, 3rd edn, Göttingen.

Goldfarb, Lewis, H. (1995) 'Trade and Competition Policies in the Global Market Place', in: OECD (ed.), *New Dimensions of Market Access in a Globalizing World Economy*, Paris, pp. 125–37.

Görgens, E. (1988) 'Wettbewerbspolitik', in: Woll, Artur (ed.), *Wirtschaftslexicon*, Munich, pp. 765–8.

Graham, Edward M. (1996) 'Competition Policy and the New Trade Agenda', in: OECD (ed.), *New Dimensions of Market Access in a Globalising World Economy*, Paris, pp. 105–18.

Graham, Edward M. (2000) 'Trade, Competition, and the WTO Agenda', in: Schott, Jeffrey J. (ed.), *The WTO After Seattle*, Washington, DC, pp. 205–22.

Grichting, Alois (1976) *Die Skalenerträge, Theoretische und empirische Aspekte*, Meisenheim am Glan.

Groenveld, K., Maks, J. A. H. and Muysken, J. (eds) (1990) *Economic Policy and the Market Process – Austrian and Mainstream Economics*, Amsterdam.

Gröner, Helmut (1987) 'Internationale Wettbewerbspolitik', in: Borchert, Manfred, Fehl, Ulrich and Oberender, Peter (eds), *Markt und Wettbewerb, Festschrift für Ernst Heuß zum 65. Geburtstag*, Stuttgart, pp. 359–77.

Gröner, Helmut and Knorr, Andreas (1996) 'Internationalisierung der Wettbewerbspolitik', in: Immenga, Ulrich, Möschel, Wernhard and Reuter, Dieter (ed.), *Festschrift für Ernst-Joachim Mestmäcker*, Baden-Baden.

Grundlach, Erich, Klodt, Henning, Langhammer, Rolf, J. and Soltwedel, Rüdiger (1995) *Fairness im Standortwettbewerb? Auf dem Weg zur internationalen Ordnungspolitik*, Kiel Discussion Papers, no. 254, June.

Hagedoorn, J. (1996) 'The Economics of Cooperation Among High-Tech Firms', in: Albach, Horst, Koopmann, Georg and Scharrer, Hans-Eckart (eds), *The*

Economics of High-Technology Competition and Cooperation in Global Markets, Baden-Baden, pp. 173–98.

Hauser, Heinz and Schoene, Rainer E. (1994) 'Is There a Need for International Competition Rules?', *Aussenwirtschaft*, vol. 49, nos. 2–3, pp. 205–22.

Hawk, Barry, E. (1987) *United States, Common Market and International Antitrust: A Comparative Guide*, Clifton, NJ, 1987.

Hawk, Barry E. (1995) 'System Failure: Vertical Restraints and EC Competition Law', in: *Common Market Law Review*, vol. 33, pp. 973–89.

Hawk, Barry E. (1996) 'Antitrust Policy and Market Access', in: *OECD Observer*, no. 201, pp. 10–12.

Hay, Donald (1993) 'The Assessment: Competition Policy', in: *Oxford Review of Economic Policy*, vol. 9, no. 2, pp. 1–26.

Hayek, Friedrich August von (1949) *The Meaning of Competition in Individualism and Economic Order*, London.

Hayek, Friedrich August von (1969) 'Der Wettbewerb als Entdeckungsverfahren', in: Hayek, Friedrich August von (ed.), *Freiburger Studien*, Tübingen, pp. 243–65.

Hayek, Friedrich August von (1975) 'Die Anmaßung von Wissen', in: *ORDO (Jahrbuch für die Ordnung von Wirtschaft und Gesellschaft)*, vol. 26, pp. 12–21.

Hayek, Friedrich August von (1978) 'Competition as a Discovery Procedure', in: *New Studies in Philosophy, Politics, Economics and the History of Ideas*, Chicago (first printed as a lecture 1968), pp. 179–90.

Herder-Dorneich, Phillip (1957) *Theorie der Bestimmungsfaktoren finanzwissenschaftlicher Staatstätigkeit*, Freiburg.

Herdzina, Klaus (1999) *Wettbewerbspolitik*, 5th edn, Stuttgart.

Hermanns, Ferdinand (1989) 'Extraterritoriale Rechtsanwendung', in: Andreae, Clemens-August, Kirchhoff, Jochen and Pfeiffer, Gerd (eds), *Wettbewerb als Herausforderung und Chance*, Cologne, pp. 439–51.

Heuß, Ernst (1968) 'Wachstums- und Wettbewerbsbeschränkungen', in: Mestmäcker, Ernst-Joachim (ed.), *Wettbewerb als Aufgabe*, Bad Homburg, pp. 30–60.

Hildebrand, Doris (2002a) *The Role of Economic Analysis in the EC Competition Rules*, Kluwer, The Hague.

Hildebrand, Doris (2002b) 'The European School in EC Competition Law', *World Competition*, vol. 25, no. 1, pp. 3–23.

Hillman, A. and Katz, E. (1986) 'Domestic Uncertainty and Foreign Dumping', *Journal of Economics*, vol. 19, no. 3, pp. 403–16.

Hindley, Brian (1996) 'Competition Law and the WTO: Alternative Structures for Agreement', in: Bhagwati, Jagdish and Hudec, Robert E. (eds), *Fair Trade and Harmonization: Prerequisites for Free Trade?*, Massachusetts Institute of Technology, Cambridge, MA, pp. 334–48.

Hindley, Brian (2000) 'Is The Millennium Round Worth Reviving?', in: *Zeitschrift für Wirtschaftspolitik*, vol. 49, no. 1, pp. 52–8.

Hindley, Brian (2002) 'What Subjects Are Suitable for WTO Agreement?', in: Kennedy, Daniel L. M. and Southwick, James D. (eds), *The Political Economy of International Trade Law: Essays in Honor of Robert E. Hudec*, Cambridge, MA, pp. 157–76.

Hoekman, Bernhard (1997) 'Competition Policy and the Global Trading System', *World Economy*, vol. 20, no. 4, pp. 383–406.
Hoekman, Bernhard M. and Mavroidis, Petros C. (1994) *Competition, Competition Policy and the GATT*, Centre for Economic Policy Discussion Paper no. 876, London, reprinted in *World Economy*, vol. 17, no. 2, pp. 121–50.
Holmes, Peter (2002) 'Trade and Competition in the New WTO Round', in: Milner, Chris (ed.), *Trade Liberalization, Competition and the WTO*, Cheltenham, pp. 147–75.
Hoppmann, Erich (1977) *Marktmacht und Wettbewerb*, Tübingen.
Horlick, Gary N. (1993) 'How the GATT Became Protectionistic – an Analysis of the Uruguay Round Draft Final Antidumping Code', *Journal of World Trade*, vol. 27, no. 5, pp. 5–17.
Horlick, Gary N. and Shea, Eleanor C. (1995) 'The World Trade Organization Antidumping Agreement', *Journal of World Trade*, vol. 29, no. 1, pp. 5–31.
Hovenkamp, Herbert (1985) 'Antitrust Policy after Chicago', *Michigan Law Review*, vol. 84, no. 213, pp. 213–84.
Hovenkamp, Herbert (1994) *Federal Antitrust Policy: The Law of Competition and Its Practice*, Place West, St Paul, MN.
Immenga, Ulrich (1995) 'Internationaler Wettbewerb, Beihilfen, Antidumpingverfahren: Von der Politik zum Recht', in: FIW (ed.), *Schwerpunkte des Kartellrechts 1993/94, FIW-Schriftenreihe 163*, Cologne a.o., pp. 1–16.
Immenga, Ulrich (1996a) 'Rechtsregeln für eine internationale Wettbewerbsordnung', in: Immenga, Ulrich, Möschel, Wernhard and Reuter, Dieter (eds), *Festschrift für Ernst Joachim Mestmäcker*, Baden-Baden, pp. 593–609.
Immenga, Ulrich (1996b) 'Wirkungsgrenzen bilateraler Verträge für eine internationale Wettbewerbsordnung', in: Kruse, Jörn and Mayer, Otto G. (eds), *Aktuelle Probleme der Wettbewerbs- und Wirtschaftspolitik, Erhard Kantzenbach zum 65.* Geburtstag, Baden-Baden, pp. 155–65.
Israel M. (1992) *The Meaning of Market Process: Essays in the Development of Modern Austrian Economics*, London.
Jakob-Siebert, Thinam (1996) 'Informationsaustausch zwischen der Kommission und den Wettbewerbsbehörden von Drittländern', in: FIW (ed.), *Schwerpunkte des Kartellrechts 1994/95, FIW-Schriftenreihe*, no. 167, Cologne, pp. 57–69.
Kantzenbach, Erhard (1967) *Die Funktionsfähigkeit des Wettbewerbs*, Göttingen.
Kantzenbach, Erhard (1990) 'Competition Policy in West Germany: A Comparison with the Antitrust Policy of the United States', in: Jacquemin, A. (ed.), *Competition Policy in Europe and North America: Economic Issues and Institutions*, Chur, pp. 189–205.
Kantzenbach, Erhard and Krüger, Reinald (1994) 'Wettbewerbspolitische Leitbilder für Europa', in: Gahlen, Bernhard, Hesse, Helmud and Hans Jürgen Ramser (eds), *Europäische Integrationsprobleme aus wirtschaftswissenschaftlicher Sicht*, Tübingen, pp. 191–209.
Kattan, Joseph (1993) 'Market Power in the Presence of an Installed Base', *Antitrust Law Journal*, vol. 62, no. 1, pp. 1–21.

Kawahito, Kiyoshi (1982) 'Steel and U.S. Antidumping Statutes', *Journal of World Trade Law*, vol. 16, no. 2, pp. 152–64.

Kennedy, Kevin C. (2001) *Competition Law and the World Trade Organisation: The Limits of Multilateralism*, London 2001.

Kirzner, Israel M. (1992) *The Meaning of Market Process: Essays in the Development of Modern Austrian Economics*, London.

Klodt, Henning (1995) 'Internationale Regeln für den Wettbewerb', *Wirtschaftsdienst*, vol. 75, no. 1, pp. 15–26.

Klodt, Henning (2000) 'Freihandel braucht Wettbewerbsregeln', *Handelsblatt*, 4 April, p. 53.

Klodt, Henning (2003) *Wege zu einer globalen Wettbewerbsordnung*, Sankt Augustin.

Knorr, Andreas (1999) 'Wettbewerbsregeln statt Antidumpingregeln', *List Forum für Wirtschafts- und Finanzpolitik*, vol. 25, no. 4, pp. 414–31.

Koopmann, Georg, Biesenbach, Peter and Adamy, Wilhelm (1999) 'Die neue WTO-Runde – was sollte auf die Agenda?', *Wirtschaftsdienst*, vol. 79, no. 11, pp. 643–52.

Kowalski, Angelika (1997) *Die Marktprozeßanalyse der Harvard School und neuere Systemtheorie*, Hamburg.

Krattenmaker, Thomas G. and Salop, Steven C. (1986) 'Anticompetitive Exclusion: Raising Rivals's Cost to Achieve Power over Price', *Yale Law Journal*, vol. 96, no. 2, pp. 209–93.

Krüger, Reinald (1996) 'Multilaterale Regeln für den internationalen Wettbewerb? Korreferat zu Wolfgang Fikentscher', in: Kantzenbach, Erhard and Mayer, Otto G. (eds), *Von der internationalen Handels- zur Wettbewerbsordnung*, Baden-Baden, pp. 219–29.

Kühn, Kai-Uwe, Seabright, Paul and Smith, Alaisdair (1992) *Competition Policy Research: Where Do We Stand?*, Centre for Economic Policy Research Occasional Paper No. 8.

Kulms, Rainer (1988) *Das Antidumpingrecht im amerikanischen und europäischen Recht*, Baden-Baden.

Küng, Emil (1975) 'Dumping und Dumpingabwehr', *Wirtschaftsstudium*, vol. 4, no. 11, pp. 513–19.

Lande, Robert H. (1989) 'Chicago's False Foundation: Wealth Transfers (Not Just Efficiency) Should Guide Antitrust', *Antitrust Law Journal*, vol. 58, no. 2, pp. 631–44.

Langer, Stefan (1995) 'Kritik und Neukonzeption des internationalen Antidumpingrechts', *Zeitschrift für vergleichende Rechtswissenschaft*, vol. 96, no. 4, pp. 353–83.

Langlois, Richard N. (2001) 'Technological Standards, Innovation, and Essential Facilities, Towards a Schumteterian Post-Chicago Approach', in: Ellig, Jerome (ed.), *Dynamic Competition and Public Policy: Technology, Innovation and Antitrust Issues*, Cambridge, MA, pp. 193–228.

Leidy, Michael (1994) 'Antidumping: Solution or Problem in the 1990s?', in: IMF (ed.), *International Trade Policies, The Uruguay Round and Beyond*, vol. II, Background Papers, Washington, DC, pp. 53–67.

Lenel, Hans Otto (1989) 'Walter Eucken', in: Starbatty, Joachim (ed.), *Klassiker des ökonomischen Denkens, Vol. 2, Von Karl Marx bis John Maynard Keynes,* Munich, pp. 292–311.

Levonsohn, James A. (1994) *Competition Policy and International Trade,* National Bureau of Economic Research, Working Paper no. 4972.

MacDonald, James (1994) 'Does Import Competition Force Efficient Production?', *Review of Economics and Statistics,* vol. 76, no. 4, pp. 721–27.

Maks, J. A. H. (1995) 'Economic Theory and Competition Policy in the Netherlands', in: Meijer, Gerrit (ed.), *New Perspectives on Austrian Economics,* London, pp. 197–215.

Mantzavinos, Chrysostomos (1994) *Wettbewerbstheorie: Eine kritische Auseinandersetzung,* Berlin.

Mantzavinos, Chrysostomos (2001) *Individuals, Institutions, and Markets,* Cambridge.

Markham, Jesse W. (1950) 'An alternative approach to the concepts of workable competition', *American Economic Review,* vol. 40, no. 2, pp. 348–61.

Martiensen, Jörn (2000) *Institutionenökonomik: die Analyse der Bedeutung von Regeln und Organisationen für die Effizienz ökonomischer Tauschbeziehungen,* Munich.

Mason, Edward (1939) 'Price and Production Policies of Large-Scale Enterprises', *American Economic Review,* vol. 29, no. 1, pp. 61–74.

Matsushita, Mitsuo (1995) 'Harmonization of Competition Laws through Bilateral Trade Negotiations', in: OECD (ed.), *New Dimensions of Market Access in a Globalising World Economy,* Paris, pp. 129–37.

Mattoo, Aaditya and Subramanian, Arvind (1997) 'Multilateral Rules on Competition Policy – A Possible Way Forward', *Journal of World Trade,* vol. 31, no. 5, pp. 96–115.

Mavroidis, Petros C. and Van Siclen, Sally J. (1997) 'The Application of the GATT/WTO Dispute Resolution Systems to Competition Issues', *Journal of World Trade,* vol. 31, no. 5, pp. 5–45.

McKinnon, Don (2000) 'The Global Economy: Continuity and Change', in: Richardson, Martin (ed.), *Globalisation and International Trade Liberalisation: Continuity and Change,* Cheltenham, pp. 8–15.

Messerlin, Patrick A. (1989) 'The EC Antidumping Regulations: A First Economic Appraisal, 1980–85', *Weltwirtschaftliches Archiv,* vol. 125, no. 3, pp. 563–87.

Messerlin, Patrick, A. (1995) 'Should Antidumping Rules be Replaced by National or International Competition Rules?', *Aussenwirtschaft,* September 1994, reprinted in *World Competition,* vol. 18, no. 3, pp. 37–54.

Messerlin, Patrick A. (2000) 'Antidumping and Safeguards', in: Schott, Jeffrey J. (ed.), The *WTO After Seattle,* Washington, DC, pp. 159–83.

Messerlin, Patrick A. and Reed, Geoffrey (1995) 'Antidumping Policies in the United States and the European Communities', *Economic Journal,* vol. 105, no. 433, pp. 1565–75.

Miranda, Jorge, Torres, Raúl A. and Ruiz, Mario (1998) 'The International Use of Antidumping: 1987–1997', *Journal of World Trade,* vol. 32, no. 5, pp. 5–71.

Monopolkommission (1998) *Systemwettbewerb, Sondergutachten 27*, Nomos, Baden-Baden.

Morici, Peter (2000) *Antitrust in the Global Trading System*, Washington, DC.

Motta, Massimo and Onida, Fabrizio (1997) 'Trade Policy and Competition Policy', *Giornale degli Economisti e Annali di Economia*, vol. 56, nos. 1–2, pp. 67–97.

Möschel, Wernhard (1991) 'The Goals of Antitrust Revisited', *Journal of Institutional and Theoretical Economics*, vol. 147, no. 1, pp. 7–23.

Mozet, Peter (1991) *Internationale Zusammenarbeit der Kartellbehörden*, Augsburg.

Nagy, Anke (2002) *Die Entwicklung einer internationalen Wettbewerbsordnung – Möglichkeiten und Grenzen aus organisationstheoretischer Sicht*, Frankfurt.

Nelson, Richard R. (1979) 'Comment on Posner, Richard A. (1979), The Chicago School of Antitrust Analysis', *University of Pennsylvania Law Review*, vol. 127, pp. 951–2.

Neven, Damien and Siotis, Georges (1993) 'Foreign Direct Investments in the European Community: Some Policy Issues', *Oxford Review of Economic Policy*, vol. 9, no. 2, pp. 72–93.

Nicolaides, Phedon (1990) 'The Competition Effects of Dumping', *Journal of World Trade*, vol. 24, no. 5, pp. 115–31.

Nicolaides, Phedon (1994a) 'Towards Multilateral Rules on Competition – The Problems in Mutual Recognition of National Rules', *World Competition*, vol. 17, no. 3, pp. 5–48.

Nicolaides, Phedon (1994b) 'Why Multinational Rules on Competition Are Needed', *Intereconomics*, vol. 29, September/October, pp. 211–18.

Nicolaides, Phedon (2001) 'Competition Policy and the WTO', in: Deutsch, Klaus Günter and Speyer, Bernhard (eds), *The World Trade Organization Millennium Round: Freer Trade in the Twenty-First Century*, London, pp. 138–59.

Niels, Gunnar and Kate, Adriaan ten (1997) 'Trusting Antitrust to Dump Antidumping', *Journal of World Trade*, vol. 31, no. 6, pp. 29–43.

Noland, Marcus (1999) *Competition Policy and FDI: A Solution in Search of a Problem?*, Washington: Institute for International Economics, Working Paper No. 99, 3, February.

Oakland, W. H. (1974) 'Public Goods, Perfect Competition and Underproduction', *Journal of Political Economy*, vol. 82, no. 5, pp. 927–39.

Oberender, Peter and Vath, Andreas (1989) 'Von der Industrieökonomie zur Marktökonomie', in: Oberender, Peter (ed.), *Marktökonomie*, Munich, pp. 3–27.

OECD (1994a) *Interim Report on Convergence of Competition Policies*, OECD Working Papers, no. 79.

OECD (1994b) *Merger Cases in the Real World. A Study of Merger Control Procedures*, Paris.

OECD (1996) *Trade and Competition: Frictions after the Uruguay Round*, Economic Department Working Papers, no. 165.

OECD (2000a) *The European Union's Trade Policies and their Economic Effects*, Paris.

OECD (2000b) *Trade and Competition Policies for Tomorrow*, Paris.

OECD (2001) *Trade and Competition Policies – Options for a Greater Coherence*, Paris.

Ordover, Janusz A. and Willig, Robert (1985) 'Antitrust for High-Technology Industries: Assessing Research Joint Ventures and Mergers', *Journal of Law and Economics*, vol. 28, no. 2, pp. 311–33.

Paemen, Hugo (2000) 'The EU Approach to a New Round', in: Schott, Jeffrey J. (ed.), *The WTO After Seattle*, Washington, DC, pp. 53–7.

Pengilley, Warren (1997) 'The Extraterritorial Impact of U.S. Trade Laws – Is It Not Time for 'ET' to 'Go Home'?', *World Competition*, vol. 20, no. 3, pp. 17–55.

Petersmann, Ernst-Ulrich (1993) 'Internationale Competition Rules for the GATT-WTO World Trade and Legal System', *Journal of World Trade*, vol. 27, no. 6, pp. 35–83.

Petersmann, Ernst-Ulrich (1994) 'Proposals For Negotiating International Competition Rules In The GATT-WTO World Trade And Legal System', *Aussenwirtschaft*, vol. 49, nos. 2–3, pp. 231–77.

Petersmann, Ernst-Ulrich (1996) 'International Competition Rules for Governments, The Case for Linking Future WTO Negotiations on Investments, Competition and Environment Rules to Reforms of Anti-Dumping Laws', *Journal of World Trade*, vol. 30, no. 3, pp. 5–35.

Petersmann, Ernst-Ulrich (1999) 'Competition-Oriented Reforms of the WTO World Trade System – Proposals and Policy Options', in: Zäch, Roger (ed.), *Towards WTO Competition Rules, Key Issues and Comments on the WTO Report (1998) on Trade and Competition*, The Hague, pp. 43–71.

Phillips, Bernhard J. (1994) 'Comments on the Draft International Antitrust Code', *Aussenwirtschaft*, vol. 49, nos. 2–3, pp. 327–48.

Plompen, Peter M. A. L. (2001) 'World Trade and Competition Policy', in: Forschungsinstitut für Wirtschaftsverfassung und Wettbewerb (ed.), *Zukunft der Wettbewerbsordnung und des Kartellrechts: Referate des XXXIII. FIW-Symposions*, Cologne, pp. 27–34.

Poeche, Jürgen (1970) 'Workable Competition als wettbewerbspolitisches Leitbild', in: Poeche, Jürgen (ed.), *Das Konzept der 'Workable Competition' in der angelsächsischen Literatur*, Cologne, pp. 9–32.

Pohmer, Dieter (1979) 'Zum Grenzausgleich der Umsatzsteuer', in: Bohley, Peter and Tolkemitt, Georg (eds), *Wirtschaftswissenschaft als Grundlage staatlichen Handelns*, Tübingen, pp. 249–79.

Pons, Jean-François (1999) 'International Co-operation in Competition Matters – Where Are We Four Years After the Van Miert Report?', in: Zäch, Roger (ed.), *Towards WTO Competition Rules, Key Issues and Comments on the WTO Report (1998) on Trade and Competition*, The Hague, pp. 195–203.

Porter, Michael (1990) *The Competition Advantage of Nations*, New York: Free Press.

Posner, Richard A. (1979) 'The Chicago School of Antitrust Analysis', *University of Pennsylvania Law Review*, vol. 127, pp. 951–2.

Pratten, C. F. (1971) *Economies of Scale in Manufacturing Industries*, Department of Applied Economics Occasional Papers, no. 28, Cambridge University Press.

Price, Tony Curzon (1997) 'Using Co-evolutionary Programming to Simulate Strategic Behaviour in Markets', *Journal of Evolutionary Economics*, vol. 7, no. 3, pp. 219–54.

Prusa, Thomas J. (2001) 'On the Spread and Impact of Anti-dumping', *Canadian Journal of Economics*, vol. 34, no. 3, pp. 591–611.

Reder, Melvin W. (1982) 'Chicago Economics: Permanence and Change', *Journal of Economic Literature*, vol. 20, March, pp. 1–38.

Richter, Rudolf and Furubotn, Erik G. (1999) *Neue Institutionenökonomie: eine Einführung und kritische Würdigung, 2. Durchgesehene und ergänzte Aufl.*, Tübingen 1999.

Rishikesh, Deepa (1991) 'Extraterritoriality versus Sovereignty', in: International Antitrust Jurisdiction, *World Competition*, vol. 14, no. 3, pp. 33–66.

Royal, Sean M. (1995) 'Symposium: Post-Chicago Economics – Editor's Note', *Antitrust Law Journal*, vol. 63, no. 2, pp. 445–54.

Sachverständigenrat zur Begutachtung der gesamtwirtschaftlichen Entwicklung (1985) Auf dem Weg zu mehr Beschäftigung, Jahresgutachten 1985/86, Stuttgart, Mainz.

Sadao, Nagaoka and Goto, Akira (1997) 'Vertical Restraints and Market Access', in: *Empirica*, vol. 24, no. 1, pp. 21–36.

Scherer, Frederic M. (1994) *Competition Policies for an Integrated World Economy*, Washington, DC.

Scherer, Frederic M. (1997) *Competition Policy Convergence: Where Next?*, ZEW Discussion Papers, No. 96–24, reprinted in *Empirica*, vol. 24, no. 1, pp. 5–19.

Schleicher, Tara J. (1997) 'The U.S. Supreme Court's Use of Post-Chicago Antitrust Theory in Eastman Kodak v. Image Technical Services: Implications for Marketing Practice', *Journal of Public Policy and Marketing*, vol. 16, no. 2, pp. 310–18.

Schmidt, Ingo (1981) 'Per se Rule oder Rule of Reason', *Wirtschaftswissenschaftliches Studium*, vol. 10, no. 6, pp. 282–4.

Schmidt, Ingo and Binder, Steffen (1996) *Wettbewerbspolitik im internationalen Vergleich: die Erfassung wettbewerbsbeschränkender Strategien in Deutschland, England, Frankreich, den USA und der EG*, Heidelberg.

Schmidt, Ingo and Rittaler, Jan B. (1986) *Die Chicago School of Antitrust Analysis*, Baden-Baden.

Schott, Jeffry J. (2000) 'The WTO After Seattle', in: Schott, Jeffrey J. (ed.), *The WTO After Seattle*, Washington, DC, pp. 3–40.

Schuknecht, Ludger (1992) *Trade Protection in the European Community*, Chur.

Schüller, Alfred (1987) 'Grundlagen der Wettbewerbspolitik', in: *Unterrichtung der Bundesregierung, Materialien zum Bericht zur Lage der Nation im geteilten Deutschland 1987*, Bundestags-Drucksache, Bonn 11/11, 18 February, pp. 58–83.

Schumpeter, Joseph A. (1911) *Theorie der wirtschaftlichen Entwicklung. Eine Untersuchung über Unternehmergewinn, Kapital, Kredit, Zins und den Konjunkturzyklus*, Munich.

Schumpeter, Joseph A. (1961) *Konjunkturzyklen. Eine theoretische, historische und statistische Analyse des kapitalistischen Prozesses*, vol. 1, Göttingen.

Schumpeter, Joseph A. (1993) *Kapitalismus, Sozialismus und Demokratie*, 7th edn, Tübingen.

Shepherd, William G. (1985) *The Economics of Industrial Organization*, 2nd edn, Prentice-Hall, New Jersey.

Shepherd, William G. (1990) *The Economics of Industrial Organization*, 3rd edn, Prentice-Hall, Englewood Cliffs, NJ.

Silberston, A. (1972) 'Economics of Scale in Theory and Practice', *The Economic Journal*, vol. 82, no. 1, pp. 363–91.

Sosnick, Stephan H. (1958) 'A Critique of Concepts of Workable Competition', *Quarterly Journal of Economics*, vol. 72, no. 1, pp. 380–423.

Staiger, Robert W. and Wolak, Frank A. (1989) *Strategic Use of Antidumping Law to Enforce Tacit International Collusion*, National Bureau of Economic Research, Working Paper no. 3016, Cambridge, MA, June.

Starbatty, Joachim (1983) 'Ordoliberalismus', *Wirtschaftswissenschaftliches Studium*, vol. 12, no. 11, pp. 567–73.

Starbatty, Joachim (1985) *Die englischen Klassiker der Nationalökonomie*, Darmstadt.

Starbatty, Joachim (1987) 'Die ordnungspolitische Dimension der EU-Technologiepolitik', *ORDO (Jahrbuch für die Ordnung von Wirtschaft und Gesellschaft)*, vol. 38, pp. 155–80.

Starek, Roscoe B. (1996) 'International Aspects of Antitrust Enforcement', *World Competition*, vol. 19, no. 3, pp. 29–42.

Stigler, George J. (1968) *The Organization of Industry*, Oxford.

Stobbe, Alfred (1989) *Mikroökonomik*, Berlin.

Subramanian, A. (1994) 'The Internationale Dimension of Competition Policies', in: Kirmani, N. a. o. (ed.), *International Trade Policies: The Uruguay Round and Beyond, Vol. 2, Background Papers, World Economic and Financial Surveys*, International Monetary Fund, Washington, DC, pp. 68–75.

Sullivan, Thomas E. (2002) 'Harmonizing Global Merger Standards: Comment on Gifford, Daniel J. and Kudrle, Robert T. (2002), Alternative National Merger Standards and the Prospects for International Cooperation', in: Kennedy, Daniel L. M. and Southwick, James D. (eds), *The Political Economy of International Trade Law: Essays in Honor of Robert E. Hudec*, Cambridge, MA, pp. 248–53.

Theuringer, Martin (2003) *Antidumping und wettbewerbsbeschränkendes Verhalten*, Cologne.

Tirole, Jean (1988) *The Theory of Industrial Organization*, Cambridge, MA.

Trebilcock, Michael J. (1996) 'Competition Policy and Trade Policy', *Journal of World Trade*, vol. 30, no. 4, pp. 72–106.

UNCTAD (1997) *World Investment Report 1997*, New York and Genf.

United States – General Accounting Office (1994) *The General Agreement on Tariffs and Trade – Uruguay Round Final Act Should Produce Overall U.S.Economic Gains*, vol. 2, Washington, DC.

Van Bael, Ivo (1990) 'EEC-Dumping Law and Procedure Revisited', *Journal of World Trade*, vol. 24, no. 2, pp. 5–23.

Van Miert, Karel Van (1996) 'Transatlantic Relations and Competition Policy', in: EU Commission (ed.), *Competition Policy Newsletter*, vol. 2, no. 3, pp. 1–5.

Vander Schueren, Paulette (1996) 'New Antidumping Rules an Practice: Wide Discretion Held on a Tight Leash?', *Common Market Law Review*, vol. 33, no. 2, pp. 271–97.

Vautier, Kerrin M. (2000) 'Competition Policies: Multi-national Approaches', in: Richardson, Martin (ed.), *Globalisation and International Trade Liberalisation: Continuity and Change*, Cheltenham, pp. 90–106.

Vautier, Kerrin M. (2002) *'Competition Policy' and the Doha Development Agenda*, NZ Trade Consortium, Working Paper no. 19, Wellington.

Vermulst, Edwin, A. (1993) 'A European Practitioner's View of the GATT System – Should Competition Law Violations Distorting International Trade be Subject to GATT Panels?', *World Competition*, vol. 16, no. 3, pp. 5–25.

Vermulst, Edwin A. (1999) *Competition Anti-dumping: Continued Peaceful Co-existence?*, Nota di Lavoro, Brussels.

Vickers, John (1994) 'Concepts of Competition', An Inaugural Lecture delivered before the University of Oxford on 2 November 1993.

Victor, A. Paul (1992) 'Export Cartels: An Idea Whose Time has Passed', *Antitrust Law Journal*, vol. 60, no. 2, pp. 571–81.

Viner, J. (1923) *Dumping: A Problem in International Trade*, University of Chicago Press, Chicago.

Viscusi, W. Kip, Vernon, Joseph E. and Harrington, Joseph Emmett (2000) *Economics of Regulation and Antitrust*, MIT Press, Cambridge, MA.

Voigt, Stefan (2002) *Institutionenökonomik*, Munich.

Williamson, Oliver E. (1968) 'Economies as an Antitrust Defense: the Welfare Tradeoffs', *American Economic Review*, vol. 58, no. 18, pp. 18–36.

Wins, Henning (2000) *Eine internationale Wettbewerbsordnung als Ergänzung zum GATT*, Baden-Baden.

Without Author (2000) 'Rufe nach transatlantischer Fusionskontrolle', *Handelsblatt*, 16 August, p. 12.

Without Author (2001) 'GE plant Zukunft ohne Honeywell', *Handelsblatt*, 19 June, p. 13.

Without Author (2002) 'Kurswechsel in der Fusionskontrolle – EU räumt Firmen mehr Rechte ein', *Handelsblatt*, 10 December, p. 1.

Wolany, Josef (1958) 'Internationale Kartellpolitik', in: Jahn, Georg and Junckerstorff, Kurt (eds), *Internationales Handbuch der Kartellpolitik*, Berlin, pp. 515–54.

Working Group on the Interaction between Trade and Competition Policy (2002a) Communication from Japan, 25 September, http://docsonline.wto.org

Working Group on the Interaction between Trade and Competition Policy (2002b) Communication from the European community, 19 November, http://docsonline.wto.org

World Bank (2000) *Globalisierung und Lokalisierung, Neue Wege im entwicklungspolitischen Denken, Weltentwicklungsbericht 1999/2000*, F.A.Z. book, Frankfurt am Main.

World Bank and OECD (1999) *A Framework for the Design and Implementation of Competition Law and Policy*, Washington, DC.

WTO (1997) *Annual Report 1997*, vol. 1, Geneva.

Zohlnhöfer, Werner (1984) 'Der neue Protektionismus aus Sicht der Politischen Ökonomie', in: Gutowski, Armin (ed.), *Der neue Protektionismus HWWA*, Hamburg, pp. 114–15.

Index